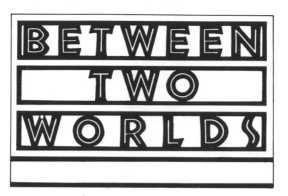

BETWEEN TWO WORLDS

The Human Side of Development

DONNAMARIE WEST

INTERCULTURAL PRESS, INC.

For information, contact
Intercultural Press, Inc.
PO Box 700 Yarmouth, ME 04096, USA

Library of Congress Catalog No. 90-055158
ISBN 0-933662-88-2

Library of Congress Cataloging-in-Publication Data

West, Donnamarie.
    Between two worlds : cooperation for development /
Donnamarie West.
        p. cm.
    ISBN 0-933662-88-2
    1. Rural development projects—Guatemala—Conacaste.
2. Guatemala—Rural conditions. 3. Institute of Cultural
Affairs.
I. Title.
HN150.29C69   1990
307.1'412'097281—dc20   90-33104
                                                          CIP

The tree symbol used in the cover design was the logo of the ICA
project in the village of San Miguel Conacaste, Guatemala.

Cover design by LetterSpace
Book design by Jacques Chazaud

Printed in the United States of America

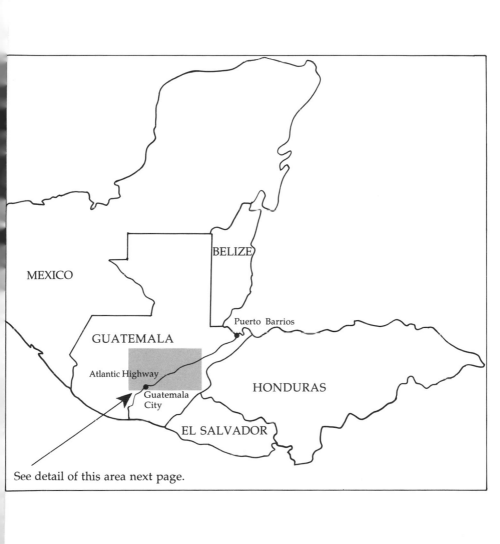

MEXICO

BELIZE

GUATEMALA

Puerto Barrios

Atlantic Highway

Guatemala
City

HONDURAS

EL SALVADOR

See detail of this area next page.

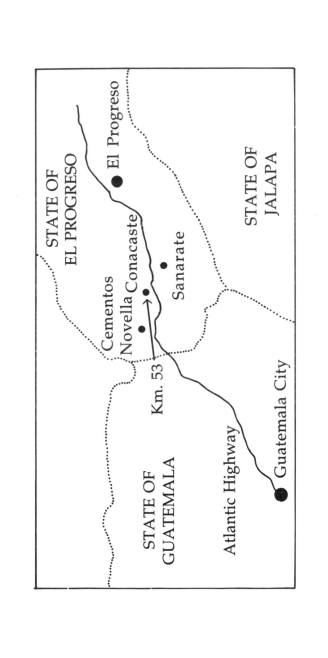

STATE OF
EL PROGRESO

El Progreso

Cementos
Novella Conacaste

Sanarate

STATE OF
JALAPA

Km. 53

STATE OF
GUATEMALA

Atlantic Highway

Guatemala City

Contents

Introduction

The thought of writing a book was never in my mind, even for a moment. I lived in Guatemala for almost six years and didn't even keep a diary. For me, authors were some lofty and special breed apart from the rest of civilization and surely were endowed with special gifts. It was also clear that authors had to work hard and have something to say. I suppose I never thought I had anything to say of enough interest for others to read. What turned me around was the absolute deluge of misinformation about Latin America, and Guatemala specifically, that I discovered flowing out of my native land, the United States.

I can remember when the sum total of information most Americans had regarding Central America could probably have been printed on the side panel of a cereal box. I know my own lack of knowledge regarding that part of the world was shocking, but it wasn't just me. One time when I tried to phone friends in Costa Rica, the international operator wanted to connect me with Puerto Rico.

When I explained that Costa Rica was in Central America, she didn't know where that was and insisted I must really want *South* America! Most Americans, myself included, pictured all of Latin America as being pretty much like Mexico—Mexican sombreros, food, music, dance, clothing, and architecture.

Long before I went to Guatemala to live and work I began to worry that in my country there seemed to be no sense that what was going on in Latin America might affect our own future. Much more attention was focused on Europe and Asia, both much farther away from our borders. Not too many people seemed to consider the possibility that the future of all the Americas might be intertwined. Today we seem to have done a complete turnaround, with our government giving the area increasing attention and the news media creating a swell of interest in the general public. I'm delighted with the interest, but the emergence of self-styled experts does scare me a little. Senators and other VIPs travel to Guatemala or some other Latin American country for a few days and return as experts. People spend a few weeks or months or years in a particular country and speak out as if they know and understand everything going on there. After almost six years in Guatemala, the only thing I know for sure is that I don't know very much. I have only too clear a grasp of the complexity of the situation.

My first glimpse of the way the United States was stumbling in its relations with Latin America came when I visited friends in Costa Rica. My friends, former neighbors in Evanston, had retired and built a beautiful home in the suburbs of San Jose. After many invitations, I finally made it down there for what turned out to be a wonderful vacation. The neighborhood they lived in was known as "millionaire row." As it happened, my friends' new neighbors had moved in not long before my arrival. The new neighbors were Russian—to be exact, the Soviet Embassy. This was the first Soviet Embassy in Costa Rica. As my friends explained it to me, the Costa Rican government was in an economic bind, so they had approached the United States government and asked for a guarantee that the U.S. would purchase a minimum amount of coffee from Costa Rica that year. Instead of asking for a loan or handout, they simply asked the U.S. to buy their product, a product that would be imported from somewhere in any case. The U.S. refused, leaving Costa Rica in desperate straits. At this point the Soviets stepped forward and offered to buy the coffee in exchange for an embassy. I have no knowledge of all the mitigating circumstances surrounding coffee imports and the international relations which affect those events, but I wonder if when we decide not to support reasonable, moderate requests of this kind, we don't often end up paying a greater price later on.

It is remarkable how life can suddenly catapult a person off in a whole new direction. A series of seemingly unimportant happenings can pile up, then merge in such a way that they make a difference in life decisions. It would be impossible to count the number of times I have been asked the question, "How could you leave a lovely home in a pretty suburb on the North Shore of Chicago to go live in a dirt-floored house in Central America?" Naturally, that kind of shift in lifestyle does not happen overnight or because of one incident or a sudden decision, although it felt that way at the time.

My life followed a solidly dependable, predictable, and ordinary course. A computer printout would tell you that I was an average, upper-middle-class Caucasian, North American female. It would show that I had a healthy, happy, and normal childhood, with the usual tension between conforming to the crowd and searching for and being the "real me." Looking back, I can see that for most of my life I was searching for a life of service in some form, but it was a vague fantasy, unclear and undefined.

I grew up in Evanston, Illinois, went to college, did some fashion modeling, worked in the delivery room at

3

Evanston Hospital, was an office nurse, got married and had two children, did photographic modeling, was (again) an office nurse, got a divorce, and then sold real estate for six years.

That, of course, is a very superficial description. In my life—as in anyone's—there were deeper, underlying themes which, in my case, converged to send me off in a new direction. What were those underlying themes?

My childhood was centered both spiritually and socially around the Congregational church. Many of my friends were from the church youth group. Consciously or unconsciously, I soaked up the message built into the Christian story—the image of serving and caring for my brother (everyone), of serving without expectation of reward, of expressing my faith through quiet action. My grandfather was a Congregational minister, and my parents were deeply involved in the life of the church—as I was. During the early part of my adult life, my service activities were focused in the church, but as I became more aware of critical community needs, my service work moved out into the more secular and ecumenical.

The massive demonstrations and open housing marches in Evanston during the early 1960s marked my first step out into the world to speak my convictions. Later, I went to work as a volunteer teacher three days a week in an all-black child care center with the stipulation that my three-year-old daughter could participate in the program. That fulfilled equally my desire to serve and my desire to have my children grow up with some idea of the multicultural world in which they lived. The center's facilities were in the basement of an old wooden church, a real firetrap. Later, as a member of the board of directors, I was involved in the search for decent facilities in an area that would encourage integration and helped raise money to renovate an old mansion that was to become the new school.

Over the years I became increasingly aware that I

wanted to do something more with my life than participate in the eternal struggle to keep ahead of the bills and acquire more "stuff." After my divorce I realized that once my children were on their own, I would have the freedom to decide what to do with my life. I gradually began to gather information about the Peace Corps and similar organizations.

As it happened, my first step on the road to Guatemala began with a casual telephone conversation. A friend invited me to see slides of a human development project in India and to hear about similar projects the Institute of Cultural Affairs (ICA) had started around the world. My answer was even more casual than the invitation: "Well, maybe I'll stop by after my shopping, if I'm not too tired and it's not too late." It was not what you would label a wildly enthusiastic response. Well, I went, and my imagination was set afire.

My admiration for the Peace Corps was considerable, but while the work of ICA was somewhat similar to that of the Peace Corps, there were some distinct differences. ICA was not connected to any government, religious, or other organization. Programs were the responsibility of local leadership so that adjustments and changes could be made quickly.

Peace Corps workers are given individual assignments, often at scattered sites. Thus, they are out in a village on their own and it is up to them to develop relationships with the local people. They are required to check in at headquarters in the capital city at regular intervals. ICA sets up an international team of people who live and work together at a particular project. An attempt is made to see that at least half the team is from the host country and that the other half consists of a mix of nations, races, religious backgrounds, ages, and skills. This provides for flexibility in the programs, better interaction with the community, and a network of moral support on site when the going gets rough. Just as important, it creates support systems that allow the team to operate out of a philosophy that centers around the concept of comprehensive development, which simply means working in all arenas at once.

The Peace Corps sends in a person, or persons, with special expertise to set up a predesigned, focused program. That might be anything from the initiation of bee raising to the establishment of a health clinic. The Peace Corps worker might help locals set up the program and conduct training and/or supervise the project. ICA believes it is necessary to develop the specifics of the project from local input and to work in a variety of arenas—expanded education, purified drinking water, better agriculture, and improved sanitation—in order to have permanent, ongoing health improvement. They believe each arena is related to others. Consequently, while they may focus on obtaining electricity for a village as top priority, they will simultaneously start a preschool, an adult literacy program, a farmers' cooperative, and some small industries.

ICA sees itself acting as a catalytic agent, a source of training, and a liaison, helping people find and connect up with the existing services that are available to them. This latter is of no small importance in the case of poor, uneducated people who, even when services are available, don't know of their existence or how to go after them.

As I understood it that first night, at the very foundation of ICA philosophy was the concept of "bottom-up" development. "Top-down" development of communities simply had not worked, as governments and agencies had finally begun to discover. Just throwing money and experts at people in an effort to improve the quality of life had proven fruitless. ICA, however, had achieved remarkable success by first encouraging local people to articulate their hopes and dreams for themselves, their children, and their community. Once they could state *their* vision of a better future, they could be aided in creating a plan to make it happen. And once they created their own plan,

6

they were willing to put themselves on the line to work for it because it was their plan, not someone else's.

The slides I saw that night were of one village in India which had been a starting point for work that spread into two hundred other Indian villages over a two-year period. I found that exciting. It was the kind of challenging project in which I wanted to participate.

Still, there was a block. How would I manage it financially? ICA was an organization of volunteers. Support for the human development projects and other programs came from grants and from donations from individuals, churches, and businesses. Some staff members worked in their professions and contributed modestly to the support of the whole group. Volunteers were also required to pay their own way, making it a double donation. I would have to donate my time and give up income plus pay ICA enough to cover expenses for myself and one village staff member. If I were to go to work in a Latin American project (which would be my first choice), it would cost me $100–$150 per month, plus a round-trip airline ticket. My house could be rented furnished and would support itself. I had two children in college (on scholarships and with jobs), and I would not be bringing in any salary while on a project, so the issue was how I could cover the monthly cost and buy plane tickets. There were no other real issues in terms of my responsibilities.

Then came the moment of truth. My friends who had hosted the slide show said to me, "We would like to be able to go work on a project ourselves but cannot do so at this time in our lives. We have some small savings and are willing to pay your transportation and expenses for the year if you will go on our behalf." Here was a challenge to the seriousness of my professed ideals.

My gut response was a strong yes, but I am not without a practical side to my nature. I understand that what seems appealing from afar just might lose its luster when seen from close up. Who were these people I would be living and working with in a village? How did I know they weren't religious fanatics or self-seeking autocrats? Actually, I had already learned something about ICA and its philosophy of development. I knew the organization was working in thirty or forty countries. I also knew it had a large service center office in Chicago. This at least made it easy for me to have some exploratory conversations with the staff.

From those conversations I found that if I joined, I would be able to choose from four new projects starting in Latin America in the coming few months. The most interesting to me in terms of place and starting time was in Guatemala in the village of Conacaste.

By its own description, "ICA is an international, voluntary, not-for-profit organization, working in research, training, and demonstration projects, with particular concern for the human factor in world development." Of the volunteers who have made a lifetime commitment to build a better world, some have remained to work in their own communities, while others serve elsewhere. They are of all ages and represent a wide range of nations, races, and religious backgrounds. The staff in each location where ICA works consists normally of an international mix of people. This multicultural approach can have a profound effect in the Third World. I saw for myself, in Guatemala, the effect on villagers when they are able to discuss problems and solutions in common with people from Japan, the Philippines, the United States, and India, many of whom came from villages or small towns themselves.

My friends had offered me an opportunity I couldn't resist—to try out the life I had been yearning for. Still cautious, I decided to attend the two-week consult (with which each new project begins) and stay an extra week to get acquainted with the resident staff and the everyday reality of living without my middle-class comforts in a poor village in Latin America. After three weeks I planned to return to Evanston, either to stay or to rent my house furnished and arrange the care of my real estate clients so I could go back to Guatemala. Some of my family and friends thought I had lost my mind. But by the time I returned from the consult in Conacaste, I had no doubts. I had fallen in love with Guatemala.

With a lot of help from my friends I eventually sorted out my life, stuffed in needed belongings, squeezed shut my suitcases, and was ready to go. Little did I guess the changes that would come into my life. For one thing, after almost ten years of being single, I was destined to remarry. For another, I would discover the richness of an entirely different culture and what it was like to live interculturally—which I often felt was like running up a sand dune, three steps forward and two back. I also came to understand how important this intercultural experience is in a shrinking world and how critical the future of Latin America is to my own country. But most significant of all, I was forced to confront myself, and it happened much sooner than I expected.

Why Am I Doing This Crazy Thing?

I am often asked why I decided to live my life among the poor, trying to make the rich and poor understand the interconnections that can give us all more hope for survival. All kinds of people keep asking, "Why are you doing this crazy thing anyway?"

Before my experience in Conacaste, I answered that question with a romanticized idealism. Today, after living in the midst of pain, poverty, and hopelessness, my response is vastly different. What happened to me one night in Conacaste was to decide the course of my future.

When ICA began the Human Development Project in Conacaste, there was almost no medical care available in the village. One male nurse with limited training came Monday through Friday during the day. Unfortunately, people seem to have most of their medical emergencies at night or on weekends. Just ask any doctor. Much to my horror, the villagers and our own staff regarded me with my limited medical experience as the closest thing they had to a doctor. The nearest clinic was seven kilometers away in Sanarate. There was not a vehicle in the village except ours and that was a "sometime thing." It was not unusual for me to be dragged out of bed or away from my work three or four times a week to treat burns or bandage a cut.

Dealing with medical situations was bad enough, but dealing with the fatalism and apathetic acceptance that went with serious illness was worse. Over and over again I would have to convince the patient and family that the critically ill person might indeed die and that they should at least go to the hospital and try to save the patient's life. We would often waste precious hours in conversation as my anxiety level and anger climbed in direct relationship to the sinking condition of the patient. It was a confrontation with this fatalism, apathy and, especially, the resistance to going to the hospital that changed the course of my life.

I had been in the village two or three months before I understood the underlying reasons for this resistance. Many of the villagers felt that the soul was with the body and wasn't going to go to heaven unless the body was buried in its rightful place near home. If a person died in the hospital, the villagers claimed that it cost $100 to pay for an autopsy and a special vehicle to bring the body home. The authorities did not let them wrap the body in a blanket and put it in the back of a friend's pickup truck. People in Conacaste simply did not have the money to pay these expenses.

But in addition to their practical fears, there was also a strong streak of fatalism. What will be, will be. Many times a very sick adult has said to me, "Well, I am not so young anymore, and it is my time, I guess. There is no point in going to the hospital. Since I'm probably going to die, I want to die at home." And then, of course, because they had decided to die, they did.

Hardest of all to face were the babies that died, usually

of dehydration as a result of diarrhea. Babies crawled in the dirt outside or on the dirt floors in their houses where a variety of animals roamed freely. Since babies put their hands and just about anything else they could find into their mouths, it was pretty hard for a baby not to ingest parasites. An additional risk occurred if a mother was not nursing her baby and used unboiled contaminated well water to mix with the formula. Diarrhea would show up as a symptom from most types of parasites. Many of the mothers did not know how to treat diarrhea and would let it go on too long before seeking help.

Standard village treatment for all illness was to wrap the patient tightly in cloths and blankets, even if the temperature outside was ninety-five degrees and the patient's temperature was 106. By the time parents sought help for their babies, it was often too late. Babies who had survived their first couple of years of life in the village provided classic examples of survival of the fittest. The project had a big educational job to do.

The important series of events that so affected me began late one afternoon, when I was called to a house to see a sick baby. I was appalled at the condition of the child and the fact that she had been ill for more than twenty-four hours. The family said she had had some kind of seizure the day before that had left her partially paralyzed on one side. She had diarrhea and a high fever. They had wrapped her up like a little mummy in rags soaked in pungent herbs and ointments. The poor thing looked near death, and the family had accepted her fate as inevitable. I talked and begged for hours, and finally they agreed we should try to save her by taking her into Children's Hospital in Guatemala City.

Before the project opened, we had visited Dr. Asturias Valenzuela, director of Children's Hospital, to tell him of our plans to work in Guatemala and had gained his enthusiastic support. He had offered free care for any children of Conacaste brought in by project staff. He was one of the most prestigious doctors in the country and, among other things, was a consultant with CARE. He also assured us that in the event of a death, there would be no charge for releasing the body.

The trip to Guatemala City was terrifying. The mother sat in the middle of the back seat of our VW double-cab pickup, clutching the baby tightly in her arms. The father sat silent, pressed close beside her with an arm clutching them both. I knelt hanging over the back of the seat on the passenger side, watching every movement, ready to snatch the baby for artificial respiration should it be necessary. It was a good thing that George West, director of the project, was driving since he was familiar with the road and, to some extent, the city. The two-lane road was not easy to negotiate as it wound through the mountains, and it was still under reconstruction from the big earthquake of 1976. We drove on the wrong side of the road and even off the road to get by other vehicles, which meant we were often on the soft shoulder and precariously balanced on the edge of the mountainside.

Then we came to the police barricades at the beginning of a long section of road under construction, with only one usable lane. Taking turns meant a thirty- to fifty-minute wait from the time the police closed the road going in our direction. We arrived just as they were putting the barricade across our lane. We all yelled at the police. A man came over with his flashlight to check us out. We frantically explained that we had an emergency with a sick baby. He flashed his light on the baby and asked, "Is it dead?" It was about all I could do to keep from screaming at him, "No, of course not. If she were dead, we wouldn't be in such a hurry to get to the hospital!" After an agonizing few moments of discussion among themselves, the police dragged open the barricade and we went tearing on down the rough, partially finished road. I was terrified, half expecting the baby to die at any moment but trying to appear calm for the sake of the parents; and I was nauseated, not just from fear and worry and the dizzy ride but also from the pungent, acrid odor emanating from the rag wrappings on the baby, an odor that seemed to get stronger by the minute.

At the edge of the city, George jumped from the car and dashed into a store to phone the doctor. By the time we got to the hospital, the doctor had already alerted the staff. One of the nurses snatched the baby out of my arms, yelled at me for being so slow to bring her in, and threw the stinking rags from the baby on the floor at my feet. The medical team swung into action. They stuck needles into the tiny, limp body, hooked up tubes to the bottles of glucose, and draped an oxygen tent over the baby, all in three minutes' time. No child could have had better medical attention. For three days they fought for her life but finally lost. We had been too late. So the small body was brought back to the village for the wake and burial.

But this was only the beginning. On the night of the wake I was called back to the same house for another emergency. The baby's grandmother was bleeding heavily. She was pregnant for the thirteenth time. Contrary to my image of a grandmother, this was no little old lady. This woman was in her early forties at the most.

That night (in the house with the dead baby and the severely ill expectant mother) remains imprinted on my mind. We stumbled down the road and into the front, main room of the adobe structure, which had been cleared of what little furniture the family had. One end of the room had been arranged with flowers, palms, candles, and statues borrowed from the church. These things surrounded the tiny girl lying on a cushion in the little white box. She looked like a wax doll wrapped entirely in white.

In accordance with local custom, the house and back porch were full of people sitting, visiting quietly, drinking coffee, playing card games. Death was clearly accepted as an important part of life, dignified as inevitable and acceptable. There was a minimum of wailing, and tears came primarily from the immediate family. All those people would keep the vigil the entire night. As it turned out, so would I.

I paid my respects to the gathering and followed the husband of my patient back through the veranda and the lean-to kitchen into a tiny, single-room shanty of stick and mud construction.

One look at the bleeding woman writhing on the bed was enough to make me want to cry out and run. She was clearly in severe pain. Upon questioning her husband, I was told that the doctor had not wanted her to have another baby "because the walls of her womb were weak."

Obviously, we had to get this woman to a hospital right away, but there was not a vehicle of any kind in the village. Our project car was in the garage for repairs. So, we sent a young boy off in the dark to ride the seven kilometers to Sanarate on his bicycle in search of the ambulance. Sometimes the ambulance was there, and if we were lucky, the driver might be there also. When the driver was sick or on vacation, no one replaced him. This made for what might charitably be called less than adequate service. We wouldn't have any information regarding the ambulance for at least an hour and a half.

There was little I could do, but in an effort to comfort the patient, the family, and myself, I got busy. I sent the girls off to find lots of rags and to get basins of water; I checked the patient's pulse and respiration (which was uneven) and cleaned her up. Then I started kneading her uterus in an effort to slow down the bleeding, praying she would not rupture. The whole scene had a dreamlike quality. I had the sensation of standing outside myself and viewing it all, almost as a disinterested party. My patient became more calm. I was able to slow the bleeding, but I didn't dare stop massaging the uterus. After a couple of hours the boy returned from Sanarate to say a pickup truck would come at six or six-thirty in the morning. So I had the whole night before me, sitting by that bed and alternating hands to keep the massage going. And what a bed it was—a crude frame of branches bound together by a lattice of cord with a piece of burlap on top that served as a mattress. There were two such "beds" in the room, plus the wooden stool I was sitting on between them, some boards and bricks that formed a shelf, and an ancient dresser with one drawer missing, which I had to squeeze by to get to the bed. Those few things filled the room completely.

The young bereaved mother had come in to lie on the second bed, sobbing quietly. Most of the time it was just the three of us, although family members checked in from time to time. Now and again, someone would bring me a cup of coffee, kicking at the dogs and pigs that followed him or her in. At one point, I almost jumped out of my skin when a rooster, secretly ensconced under the bed, suddenly began to crow. Contrary to popular belief, roosters do not crow only at dawn.

The air was full of greasy smoke from the lamp, a rather clever device made from a tin can full of kerosene with a slit in the top for a rag wick. In addition, we had a few small candles. Sitting there in the smoky, flickering light, staring at walls woven of sticks and daubed with mud, I found myself settling into a sort of sad and fatalistic calm not unlike that of the villagers. I began to understand how such a condition, going on and on, year after year, might trap people into a habit of apathetic acceptance of their situation. I was to learn a lot more about that as time went along. I sat in that little mud and stick house and my mind went back—back to elegant homes on the North Shore of Chicago, back to shiny tiled and antiseptic operating and delivery rooms in modern hospitals.

All through that very long night, my mind roamed around the world of money and power and modern convenience while I sat in the midst of poverty, apathy, and almost total lack of hope. I thought of the distance between these two worlds on our planet—not distance in miles, not

17

distance between differing political or religious philoso-
phies, but rather the distance between those who have
seen how life for almost 85 percent of humanity really is
and those who haven't. In the midst of my meditation I
had a very clear understanding that I could never return
to selling pretty houses or even to living in my own. It was
not that there is anything wrong with a comfortable lifestyle. Rather, it was because deep down inside myself
there was a screaming mandate to take responsibility for
a tiny piece of the world's pain. True enough, one person
can't make a huge difference, but you have to begin somewhere. I had found a group of people who were ready to
focus their lives on building a foundation for a better world
even if it was one pebble at a time. For my part, the urge
to serve in the Third World was so strong that I could not
have returned to my old way of life and been able to live
with myself.

There are many ways to care for the people of this
world. I would not have been in Guatemala working with
the poor if I hadn't had friends earning regular salaries,
living the lifestyle I had left behind. They contributed to
the project and paid the cost of keeping me at work in
another country. They gave me moral support besides.
Other colleagues kept on with their old lives and jobs but
used their positions and skills to help with training or to
influence people in government, churches, or the business
world. Such people would have lost their power to influence if they had run off to work in a village.

Sometimes people comment to those of us who live
among the poor that they admire us immensely, as if we
were doing something terribly noble. That is to miss the
point. It is one thing to live trapped in a life of poverty and
hopelessness. It is quite another to know you have the
freedom to walk away from it any time you choose. I always knew I was there by choice, with a multitude of
options. I have some marketable skills, abilities, and education, plus the self-assurance to believe I could do

something else with my life any time I decided to. From my perspective, I was just one of those people who was comfortable enough living in the midst of poverty in a Guatemalan village. Truthfully, it was not a particular struggle for me. It isn't that I never missed my comforts and luxuries, but simply that I was able to do without them for large chunks of time. I think my experience as a tent camper may have helped. When thinking of going to live in a place without electricity or running water for at least a year, I had the image of it as one long camping trip, and I had always loved camping. Nevertheless, I surprised even myself at how happily I could get along without many of the things I had once considered necessary.

I suppose you could say we "won" that night. At least the woman lived through her spontaneous abortion. The next year she had a healthy baby. I'm not sure how I felt about that, but the child was loved by his family, and by that time conditions were improving in Conacaste. The child had a better chance for a decent life than his parents had.

Step-by-step, I had been moving through my life with a gradually increasing awareness of the struggle and pain the majority of humans endure to survive. Step-by-step, I had moved from an intellectual understanding to an emotional conviction. Enduring that night with an aborting grandmother, a dead baby, and mourning parents moved me to another level of comprehension in which I took their pain and struggle into myself. There was no turning back.

Land of
Eternal Spring

I had gone to Guatemala, or the "Land of Eternal Spring," as Guatemalans call their country, in June of 1978. Even before I landed, I was awed by the sight of volcanoes, jungles, deserts, lakes, mountains, and a runway that was suddenly there in front of us on a mountaintop, giving the impression that it had come up to meet us rather than the other way around. Guatemala City sits on a series of lopped-off mountaintops connected by bridges suspended over incredibly deep ravines and valleys.

There is a special magic when you enter a new country for the first time; your senses are assaulted by all the sights, smells, and sounds indigenous to the place. The very dust has a different smell. The airport tells a lot about the country even before you collect your luggage. The way new arrivals are greeted and moved through customs affects your attitudes about the nation before you get out the door.

Many of the world's airports are architecturally

uninteresting—box-like with a variety of elongated appendages tacked on. They most often seem designed strictly for their function, with minimal esthetic appeal, and they don't always function very well at that. The Guatemalan airport is a pleasant surprise. It is built on four levels and simultaneously incorporates severe modern design in concrete and glass with the ancient Mayan forms. What could be very severe and cold has been softened on the outside by sloping green lawns, often with horses or cattle grazing—something you are not likely to see in Chicago or New York. On the inside are huge, lush plants and carved Mayan steles. The middle level is full of open clothing and folk art shops that form colorful splashes of activity. On the top level is a restaurant and bar where the waiters are dressed in typical Indian garb, complete with knee britches and sashes, and the tables are covered with beautiful handwoven cloths.

I arrived on a plane with four other people on their way to the Conacaste Consult. As we disembarked, we passed between two bars offering free samples of national products: one of coffee and the other of rum. One of our group who had previously visited Guatemala grabbed me by the arm and steered me over to sample the rum, a pleasant enough way to wait for our luggage.

From there we walked down to the lower level and moved relatively quickly through the visa process and into the customs area. Another surprise awaited me. There was a marimba band playing the happiest music I have ever heard, the musicians dressed in brightly colored Indian clothing and elaborate headdresses, with a predominance of red and black in the designs. From above us came the shouts of greeting and laughter from hundreds of people hanging over the edge of a giant, horseshoe-shaped balcony. It was as if I had dropped into a carnival on Saturday night. The air was charged with such excitement that I was almost ready to burst with it. It's a lot less painful to drag

22

yourself through luggage collection and inspection with a spot of rum, happy music, and a jolly crowd of people.

Our "greeter" found and guided us to a borrowed VW microbus. He explained that we had to pick up a repaired tire, eighty bed sheets loaned from the Camino Real Hotel, and the man who would drive us out to the village.

We hadn't driven far before I figured out that the rules of the road as I knew them didn't apply in Guatemala City. Stop signs were treated with a "slide-through-and-drive-by-horn" attitude. A certain degree of aggressiveness appeared mandatory if one was to move at all, and it was clear pedestrians did not have the right of way.

We drove down broad boulevards with wide, grassy parkways in the middle. These were filled with giant trees and an occasional large sculpture. The buildings lining the outer edges of the boulevard were often a dazzling white. Some were predominantly glass; one was a gigantic mirror reflecting clouds and trees. Flowers were everywhere: on the ground and on the shrubs, in pots and in trees, dripping from terraces on the sides of buildings, and bursting from sidewalk stands.

But if the colors of plant life were astonishing, the colors on the people were more so. All the colors from nature were woven into the patterns on the clothes worn by the Indians. As I was to learn later, each village has its particular design and styles. Centuries ago the Spanish conquerors required the people in each region of the country to create a special design so that they could be quickly and easily identified by their masters. These designs and color combinations became symbols of the communities and over all these hundreds of years have been proudly preserved as part of their heritage. I believe that Guatemala is the only place in Latin America where one can see such a beautiful array of indigenous clothing on the streets every day. Of course the Guatemalans of Spanish descent, or "Ladinos," as they are called in Guatemala, wear western-style garb. The upper-class Ladinos are so modern and elegant as to be indistinguishable from their European or North American counterparts.

As we moved out into a traffic circle and around a lovely multitiered fountain, I saw rising from the ground stone walls and steps leading to grass terraces that seemed to be stacked up on the hillside. At the top stood a magnificent blue and white building that appeared almost as if it had been sculpted. Actually, it looked more like a giant bird ready to soar or maybe a ship or a spacecraft. It was beautifully integrated into the form of the hill and what looked to be ancient ruins. "That is the National Theater," explained our driver, "a performing arts complex that has a small theater, a gigantic auditorium, and an outdoor theater with many beautiful fountains and gardens."

From the theater area we moved into more narrow and crowded streets. The driver described it as the old, downtown section and still very much the heart of the city. We were on one-way streets with sidewalk vendors pressed close to the curbs. They were so close that I could have easily reached out the car window and snatched up a tube of toothpaste or jewelry or pantyhose.

Indian families sat on the sidewalks surrounded by piles of gorgeous woven hangings and clothing. Giant basket trays held little green parrots that pranced around and cocked their heads to look the folks over, and one young man was walking five baby goats on leashes. I was forming an impression of a carnival atmosphere that extended from the airport into the city. Instant restaurants, quickly assembled from combinations of boards, crates, benches, large pots, and small grills, dotted the sidewalks and the parks. I never did find out if any kind of license for these structures was required by the authorities, but I doubt it.

There are relatively few beggars on the street. Instead, the people are very creative about finding ways to scratch out a living. Police, and for that matter the population in general, are very tolerant of people "setting up shop" almost anywhere. They understand that the really poor have no other way to survive. So people create little "restaurants" or set up carts to sell chewing gum, candy, and cigarettes. If people need to take water from one of the elegant fountains in a park or traffic circle for washing the dishes in their restaurant or washing their hands and face, the police don't bother them.

Some people have created jobs as "car watchers." It is almost impossible to park an automobile in Guatemala City without someone asking to guard it. The driver pays five to fifty centavos, depending on how long the car is to be watched. It is a worthwhile service as they see to it that no one steals the car or anything in it.

We drove by the palace with its green stone, polished brass balconies, and leaded windows. It stretched for two blocks across from the great plaza. At one end of the plaza was the beautiful cathedral. At the other end was the National Library. I was overwhelmed by the plaza, with its lovely fountain, its flower-draped gazebos, the old bandshell, and the swirl of human activity. Finally we moved out of the city and crossed a bridge arching very high above a river. To one side there was a cemetery with brilliant white tombs on terraces of lush green grass that climbed up and up the steep mountainside. Such elegant housing for the dead while in front and below, hovels for the living poor were made of tin boards and scraps. Of course I knew that Guatemala had poor people and that in every city of the world the poor create their shanty towns or slums. Still it was a shock to see the shacks so near that dazzling cemetery. A couple of years later the government cleaned out those slums and put the poor in good, low-income housing, only to have more poor come in from the countryside and build more shacks in the same place.

We wound up and down and around on a two-lane, mountain highway. Some sections were brand-new, others under construction. Guatemala was still in the process of replacing what had been destroyed by the terrible earthquake of 1976, a disaster that had taken thousands of lives. A bus full of people had been buried when the mountains folded over on them on the very road we were now traversing. Bridges had split apart to drop vehicles and their contents down into the ravines.

At last we turned onto a dirt road, bumped, jounced, and forded a stream. Three more kilometers and we were in the village of Conacaste. I couldn't see much because it was dark. There was no electricity in the village, just candles and lanterns. Finally, we turned down a lane and pulled up beside a house.

People swarmed around to greet us, but it was too dark to see faces. Voices murmured in both Spanish and English. Someone guided us into a dark room, where we dropped our luggage, and ushered us right back out to a table in the yard. I remember eating about three spoonfuls of beans and an equal amount of rice before we were hustled off to a community meeting. I stayed near a woman with a flashlight because it was a starless, moonless night and I kept stumbling on the dirt road. I felt confused and disoriented. Maybe I was slightly nervous, but most of all I had the gut-tensing excitement of beginning a new adventure. A hundred questions rolled around in my mind: Would I be able to contribute anything of value? Would I be able to manage this strange, rough, new lifestyle? What if the villagers didn't like me? Would I ever be able to communicate in Spanish?

We met in a room with a cement floor, walls about three feet high, and screens above. Candles on the tables and a kerosene lantern gave us light. As new arrivals and the honored guests of the evening, we had seats at the tables. People stood at least six or seven deep on the outside of the screened walls. It wasn't a long meeting; words of greeting, introductions of the "new" folk, and a few songs gave me my first chance to try out my Spanish. We were asked to give our names and tell a little about ourselves. A very good translator helped us communicate with each other.

Back in my room, I found waiting for me two sets of bunk beds, one straight chair, two candles, a pile of newspapers, and two roommates. After a bit of conversation, we began to sort ourselves out. The newspapers were put on the floor as a rug to keep us and our suitcases out of the dirt. One of the women asked if I would be so kind as to take an upper bunk since the other two were heavier and would have a harder time climbing up. I was happy to oblige as I had the silly notion that I might be more safely removed from the crawly creatures of the night. With candles snuffed I settled down for my first night in Conacaste—it was so dark—so quiet!

ICA:
Consultation and
Commitment

*T*he Institute of Cultural Affairs (ICA) describes itself this way:

> The Institute of Cultural Affairs is a private, not-for-profit organization concerned with human development in communities and organizations. At the heart of its work is the belief that long term, sustainable development happens when people grasp the significance of their lives and their potential to make a difference in society. The ICA is an international organization with 300 staff serving 35 nations on six continents. The staff are committed to living simply and helping people throughout the world meet their human development needs.

The Conacaste Project was a pilot program designed to test the ability of ICA to mount effective programs for promoting integrated development in the Mexico/Central America region.

Once ICA has decided to work in a country—which it only does by invitation—it sends in a small team to do the project site selection and what it calls "framing." Doing the framing simply means building a supportive framework of informed people among government, social, business, and religious leaders—meeting with them and explaining the project. It is critical for ICA to define itself accurately and to make it clear that its objective is to help people find and use more effectively existing resources, not to change anyone's politics or religion. It is imperative to search out the people, particularly in government, who are secure in their positions so that they will continue as connections and supporters through whatever political, social, or economic changes might occur during the life of the project. Once the project is under way, ICA must continually keep all those people informed and updated.

The next step, in Conacaste at least, was to send fourteen Guatemalans to a two-month training course on human development in Venezuela. That is an easy statement to make, but for the Guatemalan villagers involved, it was very difficult to do. It wasn't until a long time after the consult, when I had become acquainted with my Guatemalan colleagues and learned some Spanish, that I understood the significance of that commitment, the extent of their fear, and the courage it took. Imagine how you would feel if you had spent your entire life in a small town or village with few modern facilities such as electricity or running water, where you took only occasional trips to nearby towns and your capital city. Imagine accepting the word of strangers that you would get valuable training and be able to help your community and country if only you were willing to leave your family for several weeks, get on a plane for the first time in your life, and fly to another country. My friend Geronimo Rivas described the day they left. "Even at the very last moment at the airport, we almost backed out. When the plane took off, we were hold-ing hands and clinging to each other." And to top it off, they suffered several hours' discomfort because they didn't realize the plane had bathrooms.

They did make it, however, and had a wonderful expe-rience, learned about participatory planning, and took their first steps toward becoming development project leaders. They were introduced to the philosophy and methodology that would be central to the project in which they would be working for the next year. Each had agreed to commit a full year to the project, for which they would receive meals and a small stipend of Q20 a month (twenty quetzales at that time equaled about U.S. \$20). Eventually, some of them backed out of their commitment and a cou-ple proved ineffectual, but a number made major contribu-tions to the project and grew into real "giants."

ICA begins every human development project with a consult, a two-week planning event during which volun-teers from all over the world come at their own expense to work with the community residents. During the consult the community must articulate not only their wants and needs but their hopes (in what is called a *visión* workshop) as well as the obstacles to accomplishing them.

The volunteers at the consults are teachers, doctors, engineers, homemakers, farmers, and business people. They work side by side with people from the community, researching problems, exchanging information and ideas, making field trips, and talking with various "experts." Vil-lagers and consultants alike are each assigned to a team with a special area of concern, such as business, agricul-ture, health, education, or housing. Finally, the local peo-ple must design their own four-year plan. The volunteers simply provide information, expertise, and what might be termed "you-can-do-it" moral support. The plan includes actual assignments of villagers and staff to specific jobs on a day-to-day, month-by-month schedule.

This method is the essence of what ICA calls "participa-

31

tory planning." It has been so successful that major multinational corporations hire ICA for assistance in applying participatory planning to their own international business operations. ICA welcomes these assignments both because they help connect foreign corporations to the local communities in which they are active and because they provide extra income to support ICA development projects and the people who work in them.

When I say the foreign volunteers (or consultants) pay their own expenses, I mean they not only pay all travel costs but also a fee that covers food and conference costs for themselves and several villagers. That enables the poorest of the villagers to participate if they wish.

Not that the villagers get a free ride. At our consult, families who could, donated a little from their own stock of corn or rice or beans. Those who couldn't donate food contributed their service. Women made tortillas and cooked and served the meals. Men helped build tables and benches and enlarged the *galera* in the plaza to give a shaded meeting place. All over the village people doubled up in their homes and made room for guests. Also, there were a few unfinished cement-block homes partially built from earthquake relief money, which ICA was able to make sufficiently usable for temporary housing. In most cases walls and roofs had been erected before the relief money ran out. ICA managed to get enough materials donated from Guatemalan businesses to build doors, though windows and floors were declared luxury items for the time being.

Most of the participants were housed in dormitories. Dorms of course called for beds and the bedding to put on them. ICA has had long experience in convincing businesses, individuals, and governments to donate needed materials and services to a good cause. In this case they cajoled the Camino Real Hotel in Guatemala City into donating all the sheets, pillowcases, and towels needed.

The acquisition of beds turned out to be a greater victory than had been anticipated. A high-ranking officer in the Guatemalan army had agreed to loan army bunk beds to be delivered in army trucks, but the day before the beds were to arrive the officer was assassinated. No one had any idea if the beds would show up or not. Fortunately for the consult, Guatemalan bureaucracy doesn't switch course any more rapidly than bureaucracies elsewhere in the world. Beds, complete with mattresses, pillows, and blankets showed up on schedule.

I arrived in Conacaste only a few days before the consult was to begin. My first tasks were not very exotic—to prepare signs and posters and make an enlarged map of the town—but I was ready to join my colleagues on the staff, most of whom had been there working for some days. There were about twenty staff members; half were foreign and the other half were the Venezuela-trained Guatemalans.

The consult began with a grand opening in the plaza in the afternoon. There were many honored guests, a number of whom were Guatemalan VIPs. The speakers appeared in the following order: a villager to offer welcome, George West (director of the project), the mayor of Sanarate, the governor of the state, and finally, the Catholic bishop of Guatemala. (The governor corrected George later, suggesting that the most important people should have spoken first.)

The consult schedule contained a combination of plenary sessions and workshops. The workshops met for five half-day sessions and focused on the specific areas of concern around which the teams were formed. Outside consultants such as myself were assigned by ICA staff to the team where they thought we would be of the greatest help, and the villagers were free to choose where they wished to work.

ICA calls these workshops Leadership Effectiveness and New Strategies Seminars (LENS Seminars). The focus is on developing leadership skills as well as on plans of action. Each of the five half-day sessions has a specific theme and aim: (1) *vision* (where the needs, wants, hopes, and dreams of the community members are articulated), (2) *contradictions* (where the obstacles or roadblocks to realizing their hopes and dreams are identified), (3) *proposals* (where strategies for effective overall action are formulated), (4) *tactics* (where plans are developed for specific projects and programs to achieve their aims), and (5) *implementation* (where a time line or calendar is drawn up for step-by-step implementation).

One of the most effective phases of the LENS process is the contradictions session. People everywhere have unrealized hopes and dreams, but rarely do they sit down together and systematically examine what stands in the way of realizing them. The proposals session then identifies overall methods for dealing with the roadblocks.

In the workshops participants fed data written on large cards to the leader, who helped the group organize the information and chart the ideas. The data for these deliberations were drawn not only from those who participated in the meetings but from others in the community as well. Teams went out and talked with every family in the community. For example, the business teams talked with every store owner and anyone else involved in a small enterprise.

The methods used were nonconfrontational. I saw groups come to grips with potentially explosive issues and resolve them not only peacefully, but in friendship as well. And it was fun. People became excited, which stimulated creativity. In their workshop groups, they came to enjoy and appreciate productive teamwork.

As the teams moved along in the process, the leader produced charts that said, "Here is what you decided in the last session." At each step the results were pulled together and written down. At the end the community received a tangible, written statement documenting their work.

The real strength and joy of participatory planning is that when a community has worked together in the creation of the plan, they share ownership in it. No one has "sold" it to them or given it out of charity. Having created it themselves, they have a deep commitment to make it work.

One day was set aside for investigative field trips. We were all put on rented buses that picked us up, with our sack lunches, in the plaza and took us to our various locations. I was assigned to work with the small business team; our first stop was at the huge cement plant, Cemento Novella, ten to twelve kilometers from Conacaste, where several village men had jobs. We were given a tour of the cement operation with explanations of business management. Then we went on into the city for a similar tour through a synthetic fabrics plant. It was interesting but, of course, not directly applicable to a small store in Conacaste. I guess the idea was to stretch imaginations and introduce basic concepts that thread through all businesses.

The final day consisted of an all-day plenary session in which we put together what we had learned and, through discussion, created a four-year plan. The charts, reports, and other documents coming from the workshops would later be combined into a comprehensive statement to be printed in Spanish and English. Every ICA project produces such a document. For the Conacastans it not only served as a guide, it also gave validity and value to their work and their decisions. For ICA staff it was a project handbook. It was also an excellent tool to arouse the interest of companies, agencies, and individuals in helping and working with us.

On the face of it, the ICA process may not seem unique, but it is special, particularly in the context of development planning done by a radically diverse multinational group in a village or small community. Input is drawn from everyone and is given equal value, whether it comes from a high official or a janitor. Anything that might be considered useless or irrelevant will sift out at a later stage without any need to overtly identify it as such when it is suggested. Indeed, some data one might think irrelevant or ridiculous sometimes fit with another piece of information down the line and become important.

ICA is also special because of its philosophy and approach: integrated development, which means that any project is organized step-by-step, is community-wide, and begins with programs that meet basic needs. This approach provides a foundation on which to build a multifaceted project encompassing human, social, and economic elements concurrently. It is also important that ICA volunteer groups are always international and multicultural, emphasizing the interdependence and globally shared nature of the human development process.

The first step is helping people see what resources they have and how they can be used. Education, information, and involvement are therefore central in the initial stages. These are too often ignored in more formal government-to-government development assistance programs.

The four-year plan that the Conacaste consult came up with was ambitious to say the least. On the strictly human development side, in addition to regular leadership training programs, the project included adult literacy, preschool and school nutrition programs, and health education. The initial development projects were basic—the electrification of the town and the establishment of a potable running-water system. Next steps included the establishment of small industries, specifically a bakery; the construction of an industrial park building, which became a community center; and the establishment of a farmers' co-op, for which the community center became a focus of activity. Irrigated farming would be introduced through a demonstration farm, followed by the construction of a reservoir and a fully developed irrigation system for all Conacaste farms. Stress was also put on what ICA calls "identity systems," those things which give a community character and help draw commitment from its members. Finally, such amenities as community gardens, a sports field, and a children's park would be constructed, and agricultural education and health programs expanded.

Specific plans were made to find support not only from the government and international development agencies (such as the Inter-American Development Bank, IADB), but also from private companies, large and small. Funds came as well from LENS programs done for multinational corporations like Colgate-Palmolive, Kellogg, and EXMI-BAL (a Canadian nickel company).

ICA is now considered one of the most effective development organizations in the world. The concept of integrated development, the participatory planning and implementation, and the care and attention to detail in carrying out projects are all marks of what makes ICA special.

But this is not a book about ICA. I gladly leave that to the historians or the development specialists. It is instead a book about what I experienced as part of the Conacaste project, about the people I worked with, and the joys and sorrows we shared. It is about the Conacastans and the Guatemalans whom I came to love and who are so ready to work for the realization of their dreams. And finally, it is about Guatemala, the land of eternal spring, and about Guatemalan culture, which is so vibrant and alive.

Life in
the Village

*P*eople asked all kinds of questions when they found out I was living in a village. The questions came not only in letters from North American friends but also from Guatemalans who were used to a comfortable life in the city. Some Guatemalans were more nervous about visiting us than were people from the States.

In Guatemala most of the organizations like ours were working with the Indians. Certain areas were thick with projects of one kind or another. In the state of El Progreso where Conacaste was located, hardly anyone was doing anything. It was an area populated mostly by Ladinos rather than Indians. We had been told that this area was poor and less picturesque than some other sections of Guatemala. In Conacaste there was a greater sense of hopelessness than elsewhere.

In the third year of the project a man who had done United Nations work all over Guatemala told us that Conacaste was the most difficult community he had ever worked with. He praised us lavishly for our success in getting the people really engaged in the project. The time came when surrounding villages exclaimed over the change in Conacaste, saying it had been a terrible place of lazy people and drunks. With the change it came to be called a *chula comunidad* (charming community). Part of ICA strategy in project selection is this: success in a community thought of as "the pits" will result in people saying, "If it can be done there, it can be done anywhere."

To begin talking about what life was like in the village, you have to talk about what it was like to get there. The bus ride was always rather wild, but I discovered I was more relaxed if I looked at the scenery out the side windows instead of looking out the front where I could see the driver pass, with heart-stopping abandon, two trucks and a bus on a blind curve.

The trip usually took about an hour and a quarter. The bus stop for Conacaste was at the Shell gasoline station, which included a small restaurant. This was a blessing because it was possible to fortify yourself with a cold drink before walking the three kilometers to Conacaste or while waiting for someone to pick you up.

The project had a battered, double-cab Volkswagen pickup. This disreputable-looking vehicle was a donation from the Dutch Embassy. At one time it had been a decent-looking truck. Now it looked like something left over from a war or an act of vandalism. And the inside was worse than the outside, though that wasn't important because it ran—at least occasionally. By the time I left the project, the pickup had only one windshield wiper that worked—on the driver's side, where it was important. The inside door handle on the driver's side was gone, but it didn't really matter because we could reach outside to open the door since the window wouldn't go up anyway. The glove compartment had fallen in our laps or to the floor so many times that we threw it away. The knob was missing on the front, right window handle, so it was rather difficult to open or close. Also, we had to be careful when opening the back door because the leather hinge-strap kept breaking and the door would fall open, banging into the front door or anyone who happened to be standing there. What I minded most were the broken springs that poked up through the seats, causing us to sit carefully. We cleaned the truck regularly for a while, but it was useless. After just one three-kilometer trip to the highway it was the same old dustbin.

We did try to take care of the truck, but it is hard on any vehicle to have lots of different drivers. And a road full of ruts, holes, and stones, plus a rocky streambed didn't help, so we concentrated on keeping the truck safe.

We were very strict about not carrying more than twelve passengers, as overloading was the worst thing for the truck. But how can one drive by a woman trudging up a steep road with a huge, heavy basket on her head, a bundle tied to her back, a baby in her arms, and two children tugging at her skirt in ninety-degree heat? So, sometimes we wound up with a few extra people. Hauling loads of sand or gravel or donated bags of cement didn't help either.

Actually, it is pleasant to walk in from the highway to Conacaste if one is in good health, has reasonably sturdy leg muscles, and if it isn't high noon on a hot day. During the first year of the project we all walked in and out a lot.

The worst part of the road was in Monte Grande, a tiny village by the highway. It was a short stretch but rough, especially one steep, rocky, curving slope down to a small streambed which could change from dry to flooded overnight. It was a favorite waterhole for passing cattle and horses during the rainy season. Whether in a truck, car, bus, or on a motorcycle, everyone would creep down that incline carefully, using brakes, gears, and feet if necessary. Going up was about as bad. A skilled motorcyclist might ask his passenger to get off and walk up that section to be on the safe side, especially when it was slippery with mud.

Once you got on the other side of the stream, small trees and shrubs crowded up to the edge of the road. There was a stand of bamboo on the right, and best of all, a giant and ancient old ceiba tree with a diameter of at least ten feet. From Monte Grande, the road wound up and down around the curves, past fields of beans and corn, sugar cane, palm trees, and mango trees. Little houses were scattered along the way, and from the rises were some incredible views of the surrounding mountains.

Finally, there was Conacaste. Conacaste had a very definite entrance. At the side of the road as you entered town was an altar. It was a little house with no front, made of cement-covered adobe blocks, painted bright aqua, with a ledge of sorts across the inside back on which to put flowers to honor the village saint, San Miguel. For me, the strange thing about this niche was that, in a land of abundant flowers nine-tenths of the year, the saint was honored with plastic flowers. I can only speculate that it was a matter of convenience to avoid frequent replacement. At any rate, this niche marked the entrance to the village. Before the consult was over, there was also a "Welcome to Conacaste Project" sign.

The road continued straight ahead through the plaza and on through town, past the *parcelas* (farm plots) of the Conacaste residents, and over the mountain to another community. The plaza and main street were fairly level, but the rest of the village was built on hillsides. In town, the buildings crowded up to the edge of the road. Around the plaza they butted tight against each other. Land is a very precious commodity so every inch is put to use in a very practical way. In cities and villages alike, walls run along the edge of the sidewalk or street, with a door here and there. Some have windows, some not, hiding surprises like pretty houses or slums, garden patios or collections of junk, stores or convents, cars or mules and carts. They back it all up to the street and turn inward for privacy. They don't waste the space in front either. Homes in the United States show off an attractive front lawn and don't use it. In Latin America they hide the space and put it to use.

The village had no water for gardens. Dust and dirt were endemic to Conacaste: dirt roads, dirt floors in most houses, and a dirt plaza. There was no grass anywhere, and the dust billowed up when there was a little wind or when a vehicle passed through town. At the same time there were some medium-sized trees, thick with green leaves, hedges of solid green, and the plant I had always known as mother-in-law's tongue, growing five feet tall. Flowering trees were everywhere. Bougainvillea climbed over arbors, houses, and just about anywhere it could take hold. The effect created was a sort of lush desert.

I learned early to watch where I stepped, whether on or off the road. Chickens, pigs, turkeys, and an occasional goat ran loose, leaving their droppings everywhere. Owners must have marked their animals somehow. I never discovered their system, but they always recognized their own "walking property." Many people rode horses, and anyone with a few cows herded them down the main street. Mule trains went through loaded with cases of Coke and beer held by big nets slung over the sides. The sound of clinking bottles could be heard long before they appeared and after they had passed from sight.

Conacaste had four basic types of houses. The wealthiest homes were of cement block with sheet-metal roofs and cement floors; for those a notch down, a dirt floor had to suffice. Next were the adobe, some with metal roofs and some with tile. These adobe houses were in the majority, as a family could make their own adobe bricks out of earth at almost no cost. The adobe houses were my favorite, especially the ones with tile roofs. They provided the best insulation from the heat and so were much cooler than any other kind of building. The classier ones were surfaced on the outside with a coating of cement, then painted—quite handsome. Some of the adobes had palm roofs, which were the most picturesque, but palms need to be replaced about every third year and tend to attract insects.

Even more picturesque but horrible to live in were the stick houses, the next to the poorest. In some, an attempt had been made to coat the walls with mud to keep the breezes from whistling through. With a lot of effort a fairly solid mud house could be created. But many people didn't get that far, and when they lit their candles or lantern at night, you could see through the walls. Lastly, there were the shacks of the poorest of the poor, made of cardboard, tin, plastic sheeting, sticks, mud, or stones. I always felt sad at the sight of them. Yet, when I was inside one, it was amazing how the family had created a sense of home.

The houses varied in size from one room to three rooms in an L-shaped structure, plus a veranda and lean-to or separate kitchen. I knew three families that had gas refrigerators. Two of them ran stores that sold beer and soft drinks. The third ran the local cantina or bar. Stoves were built of adobe and were something like a barbecue pit, waist-high, of slightly varied designs. All used wood for heat and had a broad, heavy, metal plate with edges that curved up for the cooking of the tortillas. To say that the kitchens weren't very sanitary is an understatement. Chickens, pigs, and half-starved, mangy dogs wandered freely through many of them, searching for food on the earth floor. Many of the women kept the animals out by nailing a board about six to ten inches high across the bottom of the door that people could step over.

Other than the stove, a kitchen might have a table and some chairs or boxes to sit on. A fancy kitchen often had a concrete sink that drained out into the yard or street, but in many houses dishes were simply washed in a pan of water on the table. Some families had an adequate number of plates, cups, and spoons. Others might have to take turns eating, use their fingers, or scoop the food up with tortillas.

Without a refrigerator or anything more than old

cracker tins for storage, women shopped differently from their counterparts in the States who would hop in the station wagon and go to their favorite supermarket to load up for the week. We had twenty staff members to feed. We quickly found out there was no such thing as a large economy size, and even if you found the size, you didn't get any special economy. The village stores were set up to sell small amounts of just about everything: two or three cigarettes out of a pack; a quarter pound of beans, rice, or margarine; two rolls or four pieces of bread. In the city supermarkets were geared to the middle and upper classes and operated more like those in the U.S., but even in cities, the great masses of poor people shopped in the little stores where they could buy small quantities of whatever they wanted.

When the women of Conacaste were ready to prepare a meal, they would first go or send a child to the nearest tiny store to buy the right number of pieces of bread, one onion, and two green chilies, or whatever they needed. The basic diet consisted of corn, in the form of tortillas, and beans (usually black beans), which in most cases came from their own fields. Nutritionally, this diet was more sound than it might seem. The combination in the right proportion gives a complete protein. Other produce grown and eaten in fair amounts in Conacaste included tomatoes, onions, some sweet green peppers, little hot peppers, avocados, mangoes, and bananas. Later in the project, after the addition of irrigation, a lot more variety was introduced.

Many Guatemalans really believe they will die if they don't have their tortillas each day. The custom is to eat bread at breakfast and supper and always tortillas at noon. In the village, around 11:30 each morning, we would hear the soft, rhythmic slapping of hands all around us. We were almost able to set our watches by it. It was a pleasant sound, reassuring somehow, a symbol of life flowing on as it should.

45

In order to be ready at 11:30 to begin making their tortillas, the women had to take their partially cooked corn early in the morning to one of the two little mills in the town. The women walked to the mill with large plastic or metal pans on their heads, gliding along with straight backs, greeting each other, visiting, moving into the line in front of the mill. The generator and mill wheel made quite a lot of noise, which could be heard all over town. As each load of corn was emptied into the mill, the miller added water as needed to create a doughlike substance that went back into the woman's pan in exchange for a few centavos. As they were walking back home and talking with their friends, the women would sometimes reach up, grab a hunk of dough, pat out a tortilla, place it back in the pan, and take another hunk of dough, never pausing or losing cadence either in step or conversation.

It was easy in the village to understand where the expression "a woman's work is never done" came from. By five or five-thirty in the morning the women were out in the street with stick brooms, cleaning up the animal droppings and trash from their section of the street, sweeping it into a pile, and making a fire. They had already served breakfast and probably washed the dishes. Most people were up around four-thirty so the men could get out to their parcelas by the first light.

After their early morning chores and the trip to the mill, the women made their first trek to the well, one kilometer away. Actually, the well was just a hole in the ground. The dipping bucket had a rope tied to it; the other end was looped around the branch of an overhanging tree. During the consult we talked with the women and estimated that each one spent three to four hours every day just obtaining the minimal amount of water needed for her family to function. Meal preparations and cleanup, child care, sewing (by a pedal-driven machine or by hand), and laundry consumed the rest of their time.

Doing the laundry was a challenge. In Conacaste the

women had two choices. One was to haul many jugs of water to the house, fill up the plastic tubs, and scrub one piece at a time on the big, flat, scrubbing stone that was part of the equipment of every household. I found I got my clothes much cleaner by this method than I ever had with an automatic washer, but at great cost of time and energy—blue jeans and bed sheets were particularly difficult. The alternative method was to carry a tub load of dirty clothes on one's head the three and one-half kilometers to the river. This was an all-day affair but a social happening as much as a chore. The women walked with friends, gossiped as they scrubbed clothes on the rocks, and took baths in their slips while the clothes were spread over the ground and surrounding bushes to bake dry in the sun.

Most of the women made the trip to the river at least once a month, but some went every week. Many communities in Guatemala have community laundry areas—a ring of sinks around a tank of water, often spring-fed. This is more usual in areas with plenty of water. There are even laundry centers scattered around in Guatemala City. Some women, in addition to their other work, had to help in the fields as well.

I guess just about every community in Latin America has a gathering place, usually called the plaza. A plaza can be anything from a good-sized space of bare dirt with a few benches and a couple of trees, as in Conacaste, to a huge, lush, green park with fountains and bandshells and masses of flowers. A plaza is a place to visit with friends; do a little business; play a card game or chess; soak up some sun; rest in the shade; show off one's new clothes, new wife, or new baby; and to gather as a community for an event of importance. The week-long fair to celebrate the village saint occurs in the plaza. Religious processions begin and end in front of the church on the plaza. The cantina is on the plaza. Enemies meet there to fight, and friends meet there to celebrate.

The main meeting space for the Conacaste Consult was in the plaza in a temporary shelter thrown up for the homeless people after the earthquake of 1976. The shelter consisted of a sheet-metal roof held up by a framework and posts of small tree trunks, with a wall of boards at one end of the rectangle and chicken wire for the other three walls. For the consult, the men of Conacaste built long, narrow tables and benches. The women spread a thick floor of pine needles and wound flowers around the whitewashed posts. They made it a really lovely, airy place. Meeting in the plaza signified the importance of the occasion.

Life is not easy for poor villagers, and the people of Conacaste aged early. But as I stood in the village and looked around at the mountains, flowers, and trees loaded with mangoes and bananas, I felt there would be plenty of hope if the people could find ways to make an adequate living without trudging off to the city.

The Lighter Side

When I first arrived for the consult, I was assigned to a twelve-by-twelve-foot room in a cement-block house with a dirt floor. My two roommates were old hands at this consult routine, which I considered helpful. We had two bunk beds but no other furniture, which I considered unhelpful—until someone explained to me how lucky we were to have them. I was so caught up in the excitement and activity of the consult and so freshly arrived from my secure and insular life in the U.S. that I didn't think to connect the reported assassination of a high-ranking army officer with our borrowed beds and bedding.

In the midst of the consult another woman and I were moved into a house in the village. Normally such a move would not be considered difficult. We each had only a couple of suitcases, and the bunk beds were already in place in the house. Unfortunately, everyone had been so busy working all day that it was not until after dark that someone thought to tell us we had to move. Conacaste had no electricity and there was no moon that night. For the benefit of city dwellers, when you are out in the country with no electricity and no moon, it is *black*. As if to increase the challenge of moving in the dark, on foot, down steep, potholed roads with two suitcases, our purses, and a water jug, it began to rain—hard. Neither of us felt able to carry a flashlight in our mouths, so it was strictly by feel. It took us about half an hour to traverse the equivalent of three city blocks, but we made it after much slipping, sliding, staggering, cursing, and giggling.

Having both consumed plenty of liquids during the hot day, we started before long to go in search of the outhouse. Before the consult began, the staff had determined that they needed to construct toilet facilities for the forty or so extra people who would descend on the town. Therefore, teams set out to dig deep holes. Then they set a large wooden box with a hole in the center over each of these holes. Next, they drove four poles in the ground and wrapped black plastic around the posts, creating shiny black boxes without roofs. Roofs were considered an unnecessary luxury as the rainy season hadn't begun yet. In case of rain, you could be quick or be wet. These roofless boxes were generously scattered among the adobe, stick, and cement houses, creating an interesting new ambience to the community.

On that first night in our new home we found the major flaw in the design of these facilities—they were *black*. We couldn't find ours. When we did find it, after being scared half to death by a good-sized pig who obviously considered us trespassers on her turf, we found a second flaw—we couldn't find the entrance. We slid around in the mud, groping our way round and round a large shiny black box of plastic. We were desperate but laughing so hard, tears were streaming down our faces. Finally, we found a slit in the corner that we could lift back to enter the inner sanctum. Why didn't we just squat there in the dark, you might ask? Well, it never even occurred to us. After all, we were still "refined gringo ladies."

I went to Guatemala with no Spanish-speaking ability. You don't need to be terribly perceptive to figure out that I got myself into linguistic trouble very soon. The few words of Spanish I managed to recall from a two-year experience in high school were something less than adequate for communication. Nevertheless, being an eternal, perhaps even obsessive, optimist, I tried. I figured that if I could supplement my pitiful vocabulary with plenty of hand motions and smiles, I might fake it. Understanding what was being said to me was another matter.

My first total immersion in the Spanish language was at the consult. Skilled translators assisted us in our serious work, but during social events and normal daily activities we each had to manage as best we could. Most of my friendly new neighbors had little or no education and spoke very colloquially. Many were also hampered by a lack of front teeth (proper nutrition and dental care were unfamiliar commodities in the village), which caused them to lisp, adding to the difficulty I had in understanding them. I soon learned the truth of the adage that a little knowledge can be a dangerous thing. I knew a few words, or at least thought I did. I answered certain routine questions with great assurance. When people asked me how I was, I could say, *"bueno, bueno"* as well as the next person. But I was puzzled at the frequency of one question. People kept asking me if I was tired, *"¿esta cansada?"* Women asked me sometimes and men almost always. So I began to think maybe they just used it as a casual greeting, the way Americans say "how are you?" They all seemed to expect a definite answer, so I gave them one and tried to vary it a little. They seemed to be puzzled by my answers and sometimes downright shocked. I couldn't imagine

51

why they reacted this way until the day a bilingual friend overheard me and burst out laughing. It seems I had mixed up two similar words. The question was not whether I was tired but whether I was married (*¿esta casada?*). I had been giving answers like, "a little bit" or "yesterday I was, but not today," or "not really, do I look it?" No wonder they looked at me askance.

It was always comforting somehow to know I wasn't the only person to make crazy mistakes. A friend of mine who was working for ICA in Mexico outdid me considerably, I think. He was a Roman Catholic priest, a man of responsibility, who took his language study seriously and was beginning to feel a little confidence by the time he was invited to dinner at a convent in Mexico City. He felt he might be able to manage simple conversation. Unfortunately, weather and transportation problems conspired to make him late for dinner, and by the time he arrived on the doorstep, he was somewhat rattled. When Sister Carmen opened the door, he burst into profuse apologies, stating how terribly embarrassed he was and how sorry. To his consternation, the nun burst into laughter. She laughed and laughed and finally gasped that she didn't think so. When she got control of herself, she explained that he had said he was pregnant and was so sorry.

As for me, I decided that do-it-yourself Spanish was inadequate. It would be a good idea to take some lessons.

Supermarkets in the United States are magnificent but not nearly so much fun as going to Sanarate for the groceries. The early trips at the beginning of the project were especially enjoyable. Two people would be assigned the previous day for the shopping excursion so that they could be prepared for an early start in the morning. It was a seven-kilometer walk, about four miles, to Sanarate, so it was best to get well under way before the sun was high and hot.

About the third week of the project, Joanne and I were assigned to go marketing. Joanne was one of the other North Americans on the staff, but she had spent the previous year in Venezuela and thus spoke enough Spanish to get along. The locals found her conversation amusing as she spoke only in the present tense. But it is possible to make yourself understood that way. All you have to do is add *en pasado* ("in the past") or *en futuro* ("in the future").

During our walk, Joanne told me about life in the jungle project in Caño Negro, Venezuela. They had had to deal with some things there that we weren't cursed with in Conacaste. One was the abundance of snakes, some poisonous. Another was the undergrowth that encroached at a rapid rate, requiring constant work with the machetes. It was also steaming hot. This description made me more appreciative of the conditions in Guatemala.

We moved along at a fair pace on the dirt road, slowing down for the steeper climbs. The last steep, long hill into Sanarate was made worse by the passing of motorcycles, trucks, and a bus, all kicking up quantities of dust.

Sanarate, with a population of 20,000, had fascinated me from first sight. Even more than Conacaste, it seemed to be a mixture of centuries, countries, economies, even of reality and unreality. I could have believed I was on a movie set when I saw a cowboy in sombrero and chaps ride down the middle of the street.

The dirt road became very wide as it circled around the plaza, which had some big trees, benches, a few flowers, and sparse patches of grass. Everything was dust-coated. On the far side of the plaza was a large Catholic church, and on the other three sides, a variety of stores. Vendors were scattered around the edges of the plaza and anywhere else they could stake out space on the streets. Directly to our left as we entered the plaza and across the street from it was a cluster of vendors selling everything from vegetables to clothing, forming a fair-sized market.

We moved straight ahead along the plaza toward an

old-fashioned general store near the cathedral. The scene there delighted me. In the middle of the wide, dusty side street directly in front of the store stood a couple of tall trees, which provided a spot of shade. In the shade were parked one VW "bug," two pack mules, and a saddled horse. The scene was a clear statement of the incongruities of the community.

The general store was often called the "Chinese store" in acknowledgment of the owner's ancestry. We purchased nails, cooking oil, sheet plastic, and Scotch tape. Then it was back to the street market to bargain for onions, carrots, cabbages, and such. Each item required a new negotiation.

At first I was very inhibited, but once plunged into it, I came to enjoy the game of bargaining. Joanne explained that it was important to hold our own in the marketplace or no one would have any respect for us. If they thought we were fools in the market, it could affect their respect for the project.

The negotiations would generally go something like this. We would mutter about how the tomatoes didn't seem quite firm or as big as others we had seen or about a better price elsewhere. The sellers, meanwhile, would carry on about the freshness, quality, and the great bargain they were. We would offer half what the seller had said was the price. He would gasp and come down a few centavos. This would go on and on. We might walk away to look elsewhere and he would follow. Eventually, the price agreed upon would be about midway between his first price and our first offer. It is a slow way to shop. Sometimes we would deal with several vendors at the same time and other shoppers joined in with their opinions. There was lots of action and laughter. With our limited Spanish, it was extraordinary entertainment—both for them and for us.

When it came time to see if there was any chicken, beef, or pork in town, we stacked our baskets and bundles on the ground by one of the vendors we had bought from (where they would be perfectly safe) and set off to walk around the streets in search of red flags over the doorways. Anyone in town who had killed a pig or some chickens that day would hang out the red flag to announce he had meat to sell. Sometimes we bought from a butcher store and sometimes from a nonprofessional. There were days when it was impossible to find a red flag in the whole town. There were, though, certain days of the week and certain times of the day when meat could be found even when there were no red flags, but we would only learn about that later.

As we shopped, we also made stops at stores which had fixed prices, where we would buy things like sugar, salt, detergent, and toilet paper. Once we had completed our pile on the ground, we had to find someone with a pickup truck we could hire in order to get home and, of course, we had to negotiate the price. Once that was settled upon, we jumped in with supplies sufficient for the staff to survive another four or five days.

Later, when we had a decent truck of our own readily available, we sometimes combined our marketing with other errands in Guatemala City. There we went to the huge market where we had an enormous selection and could dicker about the price on everything. But it required a minimum of three people, one simply to watch the giant baskets we parked on the ground and filled periodically from the plastic bags we carried with us. As we scurried around bargaining, we guarded our purses and wallets while slipping and sliding on wet cabbage leaves and beet tops. The first time I was led down into the basement area of a huge pavilion to buy meat, my companion told me to roll up my pant legs, which set my stomach churning. The smell of blood never did too much for my appetite. Shopping in the big city market was rather like running in a marathon: it was an exciting experience if you didn't have to do it too often.

Eating has always been a favorite subject and a favorite activity of mine. Unfortunately, I do not love to cook. I did learn to be a pretty good cook as a matter of self-preservation, but the most beautiful and well-equipped kitchen in the world would not get me excited about the preparation of food. Thus, whenever I drew the assignment to prepare staff meals, I was something less than thrilled. One thing was certain, meal preparation was a challenge. The first hurdle had to do with light; there wasn't any. At least, there wasn't any at breakfast and supper time. Breakfast preparation started at five o'clock. With no electricity, we had to manage by the light of three or four tiny candles. Whenever possible, the members of the supper crew tried to get in the kitchen early enough to do as much as they could before darkness fell. No matter what, the dishes had to be washed by candlelight, much to the detriment of our standards of cleanliness.

The project operated out of a big room with screens on three sides plus a long, narrow room, which was our kitchen, running side to side along the back wall. The space had been donated for our use by INCAP, an agency of the United Nations that does nutritional studies. They had been working in Conacaste some months before the project began, so the space was available for use.

Actually, the kitchen was the finest one in Conacaste. Across one end were two huge gas burners sitting on a concrete slab. These were connected by metal tubing to large gas tanks housed on the outside of the building in a shed. Every morning it was necessary to go out and open the valve to the tanks. Then the gas could be turned on in the kitchen. Strike a match and you were in business. The worst problem with gas was the shock when it ran out, invariably in the midst of meal preparation. There was no meter, no way to know when it was running low, and it was a major operation to get refill tanks.

We had a kitchen sink with running water. This was possible because we had a well in the plaza, which had a pipeline up to a storage tank above our building. With a gasoline pump we could get the tank filled once a day. The pump was too costly for general village use, but the project used it to free the staff for more critical work. The water was contaminated, but we boiled it or treated it with tablets.

The only other thing in the kitchen besides the stove and sink was a cabinet of screened cupboards lining the long wall across from the sink. Not having a refrigerator was a problem, but one of my new discoveries was that most food is safe to keep unrefrigerated if reheated thoroughly every twelve hours. With twenty hungry people we were never overwhelmed with leftovers anyway. Fresh eggs could be kept in the cupboard and were used up quickly. Margarine was sometimes a problem because on really hot days it would melt and run down the cabinet onto the floor. In the third year of our project, we had the donation of a refrigerator.

A major challenge in the kitchen was guarding our food from the animal life. We chased after mice with brooms, smashed cockroaches that seemed big enough for me to saddle and ride, brushed ants off the counters, and swatted flies with anything at hand. Once I remember pushing ants from the cutting board and off my arms as I tried to chop cabbage for salad. Perhaps my worst moment in the kitchen was the morning a large cockroach elected to commit suicide in the pot of oatmeal I was cooking. It just climbed up and jumped in! I was furious and hauled it out with a big spoon and threw it in the garbage can. There wasn't any time or extra oatmeal, so I cooked it a long time and kept my secret. Our biggest enemy was a cat who came in during the night and robbed us of what little bits of meat or chicken we had. It was ages before we could find and seal off the cat's entryway.

We waged a constant battle with the budget, managing on twenty-five to thirty dollars a week and whatever food was donated, such as oatmeal, rice, and noodles. Various charitable organizations and companies in Guatemala believed in the work of the project and helped us out. It was lucky for us that we were living in a land with lots of inexpensive fruits and vegetables.

Perhaps the biggest dietary struggle for those of us who came from lands of plenty was adjusting to the lack of meat. Would you believe it is possible to feed twenty people from one chicken? We did it a number of times. That works out to about one and one-half bites of meat per person. We used the whole bird, Guatemala villager style. The only thing missing from the pot were the feathers. When I look at a chicken now and remember that even then we were eating better than most of the people in the village, it seems to me that the twenty-person chicken is a fitting symbol of the reality that the poor of the world face.

Anyway, I adjusted to the food or lack of it, and I learned new ways to cook. We all ended the first year with a little less blubber around our midsections. Undoubtedly, we were healthier for eating less meat.

But gradually the budget got fatter and so did we. Companies like Kellogg and a number of local meat packers, who believed in our work, donated beans, cereal, hot dogs, soup, and Jell-o on a regular basis. As villagers took over more of the running of the project we needed less staff and thus had fewer people to feed.

Care to take a guess what the national sport is in Guatemala? Guatemalans would say, "futbol," known as soccer in the United States, and that might be your guess too. But I think that is the wrong answer.

I am convinced the national sport is "woman watching," or "how to find beauty in any female from fourteen to seventy, and tell her so." To some extent this sport is engaged in all over Latin America, but it seems to me that Guatemalan men have developed it to a fine art.

By nature, Guatemalans are very gracious, a

characteristic that extends all the way down to street flirtations. They do have one habit I found strange and a little unnerving. They frequently hiss. When I was first hissed at—while walking in the streets of Guatemala City—it made me nervous, and I wondered if I were being insulted.

Actually, hissing is simply the Latin American method of catching someone's attention. For example, one hisses for the waiter in a restaurant, a habit North Americans often find disconcerting although a hiss is far more delicate than shouting, and the hiss carries an amazing distance.

At any rate, according to the rules of the Guatemalan game of woman watching—whether accompanied by a hiss or not—a man is to look, open the eyes wide in admiration, come closer, and then murmur something charming to the lady as she passes. The repertoire of remarks murmured by Guatemalan men demonstrates a surprising diversity and degree of creativity.

When several men are blocking the sidewalk as they stand in conversation, they will invariably split down the middle so that a passing female must walk through the center of the group. That way they can all comment on the loveliness of her eyes, her hair, her face, her walk, and her legs—all done with great flourish and style.

For the woman's part, she looks straight ahead, does not slow down, and tries not to smile. In fact, it is sometimes difficult not to laugh out loud, as some of the protestations of admiration and love are so outlandish. Who would want to break the spell or hurt the feelings of such gallantry, especially when it is directed at a middle-aged woman from a seventeen-year-old? There seem to be no age regulations regarding the participants in this sport. From what I can determine, all healthy males from ten to ninety join in the fun.

To me one of the most delightful aspects of this sport is the inclusion of women over forty, women overweight, women less than gorgeous, and women who may have had their attributes overlooked elsewhere in the world. I know that several of us from the project received marriage proposals from strangers on the street. One day, an elegantly dressed gentleman with a briefcase came toward me, did a sudden sidestep, and stopped in front of me. We were about four inches apart, toe to toe and nose to nose. He smiled and said, "You are the loveliest lady I have ever seen. Will you be my wife?" I took a quick step to the right, smiled, said, "Thank you, but no," and trotted right on without looking back.

This sport seems to cheer everyone up and creates a friendly atmosphere. It sure does beat clobbering people on a futbol field. Now you know why you see so many smiling faces on the streets of Guatemala—it's not only the weather.

The "get-up-and-go, let's-do-it-right-on-schedule" North American needs to make a certain adjustment in style when doing business in Latin America, where there is a casual attitude toward time and a certain flexibility in the way things are done that sometimes drives North Americans crazy. Before even the most urgent business can be conducted one must honor the courtesies and go through a series of small pleasantries that include the offering and accepting of a cup of coffee and a more or less prescribed ritual of chitchat. Phone calls and letters include God's blessing, best wishes, inquiries about each other's health, and a discussion of the weather before business matters are approached.

There is a special humanness about doing business the Latin American way that is very rewarding if you can relax and enjoy it. It calls for a different attitude toward time and "wasting" time. Punctuality can also be a problem for time-conscious foreigners in Latin America, where there is always a silent "more or less" attached to appointment times and schedules. If someone says he will meet you at ten in the morning that may mean noon. When you are told an appointment will be possible next week, that might mean two or three weeks. The intent is important, not the exact timing. It is part of a system that values the free, natural flow of events in which things happen when they happen. This flexible notion of time has the virtue of helping one stay relaxed in the face of crisis and may be conducive to ulcer prevention. On the other hand, if you are holding a burst pipe together waiting for the plumber, its disadvantages become apparent.

Take the Bus?

Many people are familiar with the word-association game psychologists and psychiatrists use to test their patients. If I say the word *bus*, what is your immediate, instinctive response? Mine would not be a solitary word, but rather "ball fringe and music." That would not have been my response before Guatemala. I would have said *car*. In fact before I came to Guatemala, all other forms of transportation had to be completely unavailable before I would consider getting on a bus. I hated buses. When I was in college, I grumbled if I had to make the twenty-five minute trip into the city on the bus. And that bus was clean and had comfortable lounge seats.

When I was living in Evanston, I was like most other suburbanites. I jumped in my car for any errand further than the corner. Buses were for when your car was in the garage and your friends were unable to pick you up. Besides, the buses didn't run often enough or go all the places one needed to go.

If anyone had suggested that I would one day be packed into a Latin American bus with people, pigs, and chickens, I would have considered them totally mad. In fact, when I came to Guatemala, my preconceived notions regarding transportation were thrown into reverse gear. Much to my own amazement, I actually enjoyed riding the buses. After a few experiences in the back of a pickup truck, the buses seemed luxurious. Everything is indeed relative. Certainly, there is no better way to get close to the local people (pun intended).

For those of you who have been denied the experience, bus riding in Guatemala bears no resemblance to strap hanging in Chicago or New York. Riding the bus is a series of surprises. In addition you may at any moment find yourself hanging over the edge of a terrifying abyss.

The city buses are less of an adventure than the ones that tear up and down the mountain highways, but they have their own unique qualities. Guatemala City has an amazing bus system. I'm convinced that if anyone could ever figure out the entire network of bus lines, it would be possible to travel anywhere in the city and never walk more than a block. There are no transfers. It was five cents a ride for years but is now all the way up to ten cents. There are also minibuses, which operate more like collective taxis and are usually faster. The price, however, is fifteen cents. They resemble traveling sardine tins and offer a special challenge to large people. Stuffing yourself in and crawling back out requires great stamina and determination. It is impossible for anyone much over five feet tall to stand upright. Actually, sardines are better off; at least they are neatly stacked in a horizontal position.

Bus drivers often have a helper, which is a nice service for the passenger since he not only collects the money but helps you on and off the bus. Other passengers are often helpful also. In New York if someone snatched your bundles and/or your baby out of your arms when you were standing on a bus, you would probably yell for the police.

In Guatemala City, it is just a seated person being friendly and helping out.

On the negative side, I must admit that most of the city buses are not only not luxurious, many of them are traveling disasters held together by rope and baling wire. They rattle, wheeze, screech, and roar through the city. And when the driver leans on the horn, I recommend you move out of the way fast; he has nothing to lose but a little more paint, and unless you are behind the wheel of a semi, he is simply bigger than you.

Bus drivers seem to have nerves of steel and great faith either in God or in their battered equipment. They are able to stay calm under incredible conditions. I boarded a bus one day that appeared to be on fire. The engine was pouring out black, greasy smoke. Since neither the driver nor the passengers seemed unduly concerned, I tossed the money in the general direction of the driver because I could barely see him and hurried to find a seat handy to the rear exit, just in case things got too hot.

The real adventure comes when you take the bus out into the countryside. In the first place, while city drivers decorate their buses, the country drivers usually get more wildly creative. The combination of artifacts is sometimes mind-boggling: ball fringe, bells, baby shoes, Christmas tinsel, the crucifix, Playboy centerfolds, family portraits, and messages written in English and Spanish (the English messages may have come from the United States with the bus). The messages are a mixture of prayers, political propaganda, ads, and warnings that the bus drivers are not responsible for your forgotten packages. This cluttered gaiety is almost always enhanced by loud, celebratory music—sometimes pop songs, but more often marimba bands. Riding the bus usually gave me the feeling I was attending a party.

It takes a while to learn the ropes. For the first three years, I went to the "terminal" to catch the bus to Conacaste. This terminal was not a building; it was actually just a couple of blocks where the buses gather in order to compete for your patronage and to load up. The trouble was that the drivers would say they were leaving right away, now, so I would get on, pay my money, and we would pull out—maybe an hour later. I finally learned the trick. I would look for a crowded bus that I had to squeeze on. Buses left when they couldn't cram anyone or anything else in or on top. Better yet, in the third year I discovered that all the buses going out our highway drove down Eleventh Avenue. It was possible to walk anywhere along that street and flag them down. Generally, they couldn't resist stuffing in just one more person.

The number of people that can be packed into one bus is amazing. Seats on either side of the aisle built for two usually hold three adults and maybe two or three children on their laps. But why waste good space in the aisle? A seventh person wedges in the middle, where it is an advantage to be on the hippy side—broad in the beam, that is—because you are really just sitting on air. More than once the jogging of the bus landed me on the floor. You need to be wedged in tightly for safety's sake. It does get sporting when the driver's helper climbs through that solid mass of humanity to check tickets or collect fares.

The top is loaded with enormous baskets, furniture, animals, and huge bundles encased in plastic and what appear to be fishing nets. Very long pipes, boards, or irrigation tubing may be lying on the floor of the aisle, and baskets under the feet are filled with baby chicks who are too tiny to survive the wind up on top.

There were times when I thought I had seen everything. But then something new would happen. Bouncing along one day, half asleep, I heard an odd sound. I couldn't identify it or tell where it was coming from. It seemed to be next to me, but there was only a woman with a bundle on her lap. A little later, the bundle lifted its head out from under the woman's left breast and gave me a good look. Apparently, I passed muster because the duck tucked its head back under and was transformed into a bundle as before.

The most exciting show on the bus comes when the bus starts up with the driver's assistant still on top. Generally, the minute the young man has dropped the last bundle on the ground, he shouts to get going. The bus takes off with a great jerk and roar as the young acrobat swings off the roof with a flip down the side and into either the open door or the first open window. I kept thinking we'd lose one of these daring young men on a sharp curve sometime, but their luck held.

Lots of buses break down on the highway. For a long time I had the good luck not to be on one that did, but the day of reckoning came twice in one week. The second time was by far the more interesting experience.

We came to a stop with a loud bang. As it was a hot afternoon, everyone piled out quickly to search for some shade and to consult with the driver and each other. The diagnosis, shouted from under the bus, was not very hopeful. I struck up a conversation with a young couple, and we agreed to pool resources and flag down a truck. It had to be a truck because my friends were bringing home their new dining set, which was tied on the top of the bus. Guatemalans are always ready to give a cheerful, helping hand, so the table and six chairs had soon been hauled down. Just as quickly, we soon made arrangements with the driver of a big, almost empty, high, slat-sided, open truck to take us on. So for the astounding price of fifty cents, I found myself seated in a pleasant conversational group around a plastic-and-chrome dining table as we roared down the highway.

Latin American music, especially marimba music, will always be a catalyst for memories of my bus-riding days. Two or three notes and the image of a Guatemalan bus will pop into my mind, the cheerful, jingling music rising above the roaring muffler, quacking ducks, noisy children, chirping chicks, and shouting driver's helper.

Dawn's Early Light

*T*his phrase from our national anthem took on a new meaning in Conacaste. Instead of looking to see if our flag was still there, we were facing the challenge of getting ready for appointments in the city and doing it, for the first year and a half, without benefit of electricity. That first year my roommate, Judy, and I were assigned to go to Guatemala City to search for funds and materials at least three or four times a week. This entailed getting up at four-thirty, fumbling around in the dark for clothes and makeup, grabbing a cup of coffee, and walking or riding the three kilometers to the highway to get the bus. We had to be appropriately coifed and attired to present the project's case to Guatemalan business and government leaders. If they donated money, that was great, but more often we would get donations of their products and/or services. For instance, Judy was assigned to work with a group of villagers to set up a bakery as a small business venture. She went to the general manager of a large Guatemalan flour mill and got a good-sized donation of flour to help get the bakery started. Another company donated shortening. All of our staff went out on such calls at least occasionally, and often six or eight of us would go into the city together. We would fan out, make our calls, set up further appointments, and regroup at lunch to organize ourselves for the afternoon. At the end of the day we would try to catch the same bus back to the Shell station, from which we would walk together (or hitch rides) to the village.

At four-thirty in the morning, without so much as a street light to put a reflective glow in the sky, it is super dark in Conacaste. By some miracle I made it through that year without ever putting my lipstick or eye shadow on the wrong places. My roommate was also talented. She was able to apply makeup base evenly by the light of two tiny candles and a small kerosene lantern. Matching or examining clothes in the dark—when we had forgotten to lay them out the evening before—was nearly impossible. We sometimes had unpleasant surprises when the dawning light revealed forgotten grease stains, weird color combinations, and runs in stockings.

But even if we started out in fine shape, there was no guarantee we would arrive that way. Sometimes when we were wearing white or very light colors, we would dress with our clothes inside out (since the buses were very dirty) and go into a restroom to turn them right side out after reaching the city.

Sometimes events took control. One day I arrived with my pantyhose in shreds because a staff member who kindly offered to give us a ride to the highway on his motorcycle drove too close to some shrubs. There was no time to turn back, and since the appointment was at eight, there was no place to buy a replacement. So I went to the office of a corporation president (whose hoped-for contribution was critical to the project) looking as if I had been attacked by a wildcat. I apologized and explained my appearance as briefly as possible, and then the president learned across his desk and said, "You came by motorcycle and bus from a village?" We usually explained that we lived in the village because it is basic ICA philosophy to do so and to share the general lifestyle of the community in which we are working. I had noticed that most of the business executives preferred not to hear in any detail about how we lived, so we generally made light of it in a brief explanation. But there I was, in tatters in front of the man's desk, and it seemed to send a very strong message. He was so thunderstruck by the degree of our commitment, he offered to give us money before we asked for it.

Although we joked with one another about showing up at appointments in shreds, we were aware that our effectiveness both inside and outside the village was heightened by the demonstration that it was possible to appear clean and neatly dressed, even while living in poverty under difficult conditions. The poorest villagers know this. When they go to the city they look sharp. What their city cousins may forget is that being neat is nowhere near as easy for rural people as it is for them.

One of my favorite stories about dressing in the dark comes from a colleague. She had completed a lengthy and important session at one of the embassies, where she had been received quite graciously. As she was leaving, she asked permission to use the restroom. While washing her hands, she looked up in the mirror and to her horror saw she had three bright red blobs of lipstick on each cheek that she had meant to blend into softly rouged color. Instead of looking like a serious professional, she looked like a clown. Her hosts demonstrated clearly why they were called diplomats.

Moonlight
over Conacaste

*F*rom the time of our earliest serious conversations about how we would research problems and develop strategies designed to get electricity into Conacaste, I experienced some painful little psychic twitches, commonly referred to as mixed emotions.

Clearly, electrification was properly the first direct, major target of the project. To the best of my knowledge, we had 100 percent agreement on that from both villagers and foreign staff. My mixed emotions had to do with a new kind of beauty I had been introduced to in the village. My reaction was entirely selfish.

When I first arrived in Conacaste, the nights were so black I learned to be very careful about locating my flashlight before the sun dropped behind the mountain. But the blackness wasn't permanent. One night a new crescent moon appeared among the incredible sparkling stars, and each night it grew larger until a full moon lit up the night sky. When it did, day's end became the most delightful part of each twenty-four hours.

All my life I had seen the moon and the stars in the dimming glare of an electricity-powered earth. Even when camping, cars with lights passed nearby, other campers used kerosene lanterns, state parks had lights, and towns were generally not far away, all affecting the sky more than I had realized. When that huge, silvery ball crept up over the edge of a mountain, we could see well enough to walk around in the streets, and we did. On very dark nights, people tended to disappear into their houses early, but when there was a bright moon in the sky, the streets were full of people visiting in the deliciously cool evening air. As the moon moved higher, the village became more and more beautiful. The rich blackness of the shadows intensified in contrast to the areas in moonlight. Houses, trees, and people cut sharper images than they did in the sunlight. By eleven the shadows shortened, and the streets seemed almost as bright as day. Everything was light and yet soft and velvety. Like most of the inhabitants of the village, including the cats and dogs, I resisted going to bed, or even into the house.

On nights like that I discovered that I enjoyed long walks out to the far side of town. Sometimes I went alone, sometimes with one or more friends. Fireflies winked and waltzed all around us. When we walked in silence, it was possible to hear the night sounds—tiny, scurrying animals rustling the corn, gentle breezes whooshing through the leaves of the mango trees, pigs grunting in their sleep, insects making strange calling sounds. Sometimes we would sing quietly—old-fashioned, romantic, or sentimental songs seemed to be the instinctive choice. These moments reminded me of a long-ago childhood of capturing fireflies in a jar or of scooting across the grass in bare feet while grown-ups sat in lawn chairs.

When electricity came, so would streetlights, TV, ceiling lights, pumps, record players, and radios. Progress would come to Conacaste. All of that was imperative if Conacaste was to join the twentieth century. I wanted it for the village, but there was a little sadness in me for what would be lost. Of course, the moon would still shine over Conacaste, and the stars would still sparkle—only a little less brightly.

Wire Them Up!

Considering my love of the unspoiled nights in Conacaste, it was ironic that I was called upon to play an active role in the wiring up of the town toward the end of the first year of the project. For nine months, other members of our staff, along with some of the villagers, had been negotiating with the mayor of the municipality, the governor of the state, and the officials of INDE (the government-owned electric company) to bring electricity to the village. They had waded through the red tape, written countless letters, and attended countless meetings.

At last the work and patience of all those people paid off. Money was collected and disbursed. Permits were granted. Cement poles for the street lights had been dropped along the road from the highway. Excitement was high. We were ready for electrification. Well, almost.

As INDE explained, "We will put the wiring to the houses when the houses themselves are wired. Now we must order the entrance meters. For how many houses do we need them? One hundred and twenty houses? We've never had so many at once. Let us know when they are wired."

So who do you suppose was going to wire those houses? We were, and that's how we (twenty staff members) found ourselves in "Basic Electricity 101." First, we had to create a place on the outside of each house to hang the entrance meter. Next, we bored holes through the wall, and then we strung up wires from the meter area through the house, winding them around little ceramic spools to the place for the ceiling light. A one-room house would have only one light. Larger houses might put a light in each of the rooms. Concealed wiring was an esthetic ideal not given any consideration in the village. Each household was given a shopping list of materials to buy. They also had a promise that a two-person team from the project would do the actual wiring job. Families signed up on an appointment sheet so they would know exactly when to be prepared for their wiring team.

During the time villagers and project staff were making preparations, INDE was setting the cement poles in the ground. They dug deep holes, putting boards or a large rock on top as a cover to keep from losing any curious children. Then they picked up one pole at a time with a sort of crane while six or eight men guided the pole, tilted it into a hole, and raised it. There was, not surprisingly, a good-sized crowd watching at all times.

Everything was moving along smoothly. Poles were standing in their holes along the entrance road, around the plaza, and halfway down the main street. Small crews of men were packing dirt around the bases. Suddenly there were screams and laughter from the area where the INDE team was getting ready to drop the next pole. We ran up the road to see what was going on. In the time between removing the cover from the hole and placing the pole in position, a curious pig had fallen in and was squealing loudly. He could not climb up the straight sides of the hole and it was impossible to get a rope on him. Finally, the skinniest man in the crowd was lowered headfirst into the hole and was held by his feet while he tried to get a firm grip on the hysterical pig. It wasn't easy, but finally they emerged into the sunlight amidst cheers and applause.

A young Peruvian man and I were teamed up as electricians. Since he had been one of our wiring instructors, I had hopes we wouldn't make any disastrous errors. At the first stop on our customer list, the people were missing an item, so we arranged to wire them the next day and moved on. The second place was an adobe house, two houses really, each with only one room. We nailed up a foot-square board on the outside of one of the houses for mounting the meter, drilled our holes through the wall, strung our wires, installed a fluorescent light fixture, and moved on to the second house. It took lots of wire, but there were no problems. It did seem incongruous, however, to be putting up a fluorescent tube light in an adobe house with no floor or glass in the windows. (Most people selected fluorescent lighting because it gave them more light at a lower cost than regular bulbs.)

The third house presented a new challenge. We walked up to the wall to mount the backing board for the meter, looked at the wall and each other, and began to laugh. The wall was constructed of sticks and mud. If we hit it with a hammer to nail up the board, it would most likely collapse into a heap at our feet. After a bit of consultation we went on a search for some long screws and a second board. We drilled matching holes in the boards, then took up positions on each side of the wall and managed to screw the boards to each other through the wall. It worked, and on we went with the wiring.

We completed the one hundred and twenty houses in about three weeks. Then we reported to INDE that we were ready for the meters. Six months later, the meters arrived and we were ready to turn on the lights in Conacaste.

I'm sure any reputable electrical inspector would have been upset by our amateur work. But in the three years since installation there have been no electrical fires or electrocutions in Conacaste. The lights worked. When I last passed that mud house, they still had the same wall, and the meter was still hanging on its original mounting.

What a night that was when they turned on the lights in Conacaste. The plaza was packed with excited people. There were speeches, marimba music, and refreshments. Then, at last, the time came to throw the switch. On flashed the street lights, the house lights, and the tiny, multicolored lights decorating the plaza. And from the people there rose one giant, simultaneous "ahhhhhhhh." Conacaste was finally wired up to the rest of the world and to the twentieth century.

The Women
of Conacaste

Women have sometimes been called the weaker sex, but the phrase doesn't fit the women of Conacaste. After the first few months of living in Guatemala, it became clear that these women were not only strong physically, they had a strength of will and a kind of courage which often outstrips their female cousins to the north.

Women play a particularly important part in the pre-schools which are among the first things set up by ICA in both urban and rural projects. Setting up a school is a fairly safe way to begin making changes as there is not likely to be opposition. But in accordance with its philosophy, ICA did not establish preschool programs for a community. The community had to be prepared to take on the responsibility itself. ICA was ready to help train staff and provide the backup assistance necessary to create good schools, but it did so strictly from behind the scenes.

At the consult in Conacaste slides were shown which included wonderful pictures of preschoolers in other projects like Fifth City in Chicago as well as projects in the Philippines and in India. The Guatemalans adore and value children and thus especially enjoyed seeing these youngsters demonstrating their skills. They also asked a lot of questions. During the discussion it became clear that they assumed ICA or the national governments involved had paid for the preschool program, providing teachers and buying uniforms and materials. This gave ICA another opportunity to emphasize that it was not a giveaway organization. ICA was ready to help the community develop educational programs but only if the people there made the decision themselves and assumed responsibility for the program.

One of our staff members, Priscilla, was a volunteer from an ICA project in Venezuela, Caño Negro. As a Caño Negro villager, she had been given training and had worked in the preschool there. Priscilla, with her snapping eyes, broad smile, and wiry, slender body, was a bundle of energy. She was a black, female version of the Pied Piper. She attracted children as surely as filings are drawn to a magnet. They draped themselves over her and followed her through the streets, prancing around her as she walked. She was a natural for assignment to the preschool program. Other people with more formal training and experience were also assigned to work in the school at various times, but eighteen-year-old Priscilla definitely had her special gifts to offer. And precisely because she was from a small, poor village herself and had so little formal education, she was a wonderful role model for the women of Conacaste.

With Priscilla as a catalyst, the parents of Conacaste decided to have a preschool. Owners of a cement-block house agreed to allow it to be used as a school for one year in exchange for the installation of a floor and doors. That was all that was needed. The nearby company, Cemento Novella, donated cement for the floor, and the men of the village contributed their labor to lay the floor and build doors. The cement company was a boon, regularly donating both money and cement to the project. However, it was the women of the village who took responsibility for implementing the project over the long term. Several volunteered to train as teachers. Others offered to sew uniforms. After some role-playing practice two of the women went to the city with our staff to visit fabric stores and ask for donations of yardage. They talked to store managers, describing the four-year plan created by the village and the details of how they would operate the preschool. They won the support of enough people to return to the village with fabric for the uniforms, and they were beaming with pride as they staggered in with armfuls of peach-and-white checkered material.

At the end of the year when the house was turned back to the owners, some of the mother-teachers decided to allow part of their homes to be used as schoolrooms. That was no small sacrifice since the schoolroom space often occupied as much as half of the family living quarters. That decision also led to decentralization. We eventually had smaller schools in four different sectors of town. In time we found money for tiny salaries.

The real importance of the preschools became apparent after the children "graduated" and entered the elementary school. The elementary schoolteachers, who came from outside the community to teach (one from the capital and the other from Sanarate), were skeptical about the value of the preschools until they began to discover the direct results in their classrooms. Since there had been no kindergarten, children had gone right into first grade to begin reading and writing—with all the problems related to being unprepared. Now the teachers found that the children were ready to learn, that they could sit still in the classroom and concentrate on studying, and that they could function effectively with their peers. The more subtle results showed up in the community attitude toward education. The word education began to take on new meaning for the village. More parents brought their children to pre-school. The nighttime literacy classes for adults increased in size and began to graduate more and more people. And none too soon. The newly formed farmers' cooperative was going to need leaders who could read and write and keep books. People began to understand that education could lead to a better life for themselves and their children. With the change of attitude, children stayed in school longer. Some parents made the necessary sacrifices to send their children to high school in Sanarate. No one had gone to secondary school in years from Conacaste. And in the fourth year, the volunteer teachers of the preschools taught class in the morning and went to class in the after-noon.

From the first year we had a fairly constant trickle of inquiries from surrounding villages as to how they could do a project, including inquiries not only about how to get electricity, drip irrigation, and a potable water system, but also about how to start a preschool. A great moment of victory for Conacaste women came when the teacher-mothers decided to enter into a serious training program to equip them to train women of other villages to set up schools and teach.

When it came to physical strength, my Conacaste sis-ters, who, in all probability, had not enjoyed the good nutrition I had, put me to shame. My "house and garden" life on the North Shore of Lake Michigan had been physi-cally active, but it was nothing in comparison to digging wells, latrines, or ditches for pipeline. Shoveling sand and gravel and hauling water and rocks were also new to my exercise regimen. I began to develop muscle strength, but I could never catch up with the Guatemalans. I used to watch the village women pick up huge baskets of fruit or heavy jugs of water, and with quick, light flips settle the load gently and securely on top of their heads. The shape, size, or weight of an object didn't seem to matter. One day a group of us were moving mattresses from a pickup truck to a house a half-block from the road. I watched as one after another of the village women hoisted a mattress on top of her head and trotted down the hill. It looked easy but it wasn't, at least not for me. I managed to get one on my head, but both the mattress and I were off balance and tipped forward into a treacherous downhill roll. I was saved from disaster by a woman who grabbed my belt loop and yanked me back to the edge of the road.

Another time I was staggering down the street with a jug of water. I tried wrapping both arms around it and hugging it to my chest. I tried holding it with one hand at a time by the handle, alternating sides, and then I tried the "stick out the hip" method. Every few yards I tried a new position or set the jug on the ground for a moment's rest. To my consternation I saw one of my neighbors watching me. Finally, as I got near her house she shrugged and came running out to meet me. As she whisked the jug out of my arms and onto her head, she chuckled and called me her "poor little kitten." I walked along beside her, feeling foolish all the way to my own doorstep, where she set the jug on the ground, gave me a toothless grin, and told me I needed to learn to use my head.

I found the physical strength of the village women amazing, especially when they were five feet tall or less and probably couldn't hit ninety pounds on the scale soaking wet. And it wasn't just their strength that was surprising but their endurance also. The village decided to spell out CONACASTE near the mountaintop behind the village. The villagers carried up large rocks, laid them out to form the letters, and whitewashed them. The staff joined the villagers in finding rocks and carrying them one at a time up the steep mountainside. I finally made it to the top with one rock, which I turned over to the people who were forming letters and painting them, and then I dropped to the ground in exhaustion. While I lay there, a wiry little old woman came trotting up and set down a rock considerably bigger than mine. She didn't even look tired. When she turned to go back down, I asked her if she wanted to rest a minute. She said, "No, I'm not tired, and if I hurry, I might get two or three more stones up before I go to the river to wash clothes." I refrained from asking how many rocks she had already carried up.

The Conacaste women outshone me just as surely in the fields as they had in the rock-carrying project. When I picked little cucumbers under the searing sun in the demonstration farm fields, I wore gloves because the fuzzy, prickly surface vines gave my skin a red, raw rash that itched and burned. I picked slowly, and my back ached painfully after only an hour of bending. The Guatemalan women, on the other hand, went gliding down the rows with the ease of suburban housewives plucking products off the shelves at the local supermarket.

The Conacaste women were lively in conversation with other women, and in small groups they expressed their opinions, but at community meetings with the men present they rarely said a word. We knew they had good ideas, but they didn't seem able to speak up and share them. We needed a way to break through their inhibitions about speaking out in meetings with the men.

One of the programs developed by ICA is called the Global Women's Forum. It was designed to be for, about, and by women. The structure of it is such that it stimulates honest conversation among women, even though they may come from very diverse backgrounds. Our staff in Guatemala learned that a team of women from the States was going to be traveling in Latin America with the Global Women's Forum program, and we asked to be put on their itinerary.

When we announced at the community meeting that there was to be a special program just for women (and to honor the women as special guests), the response from the men was snickers and smiles of disbelief. I suspect they simply did not believe us when we said they would be excluded. There was no need to press the point, however, since they would find out for themselves when the day came. The program would take place in the pavilion in the plaza, where the consult had been held, and the women on our staff would be hostesses. The Guatemalan staff members, Odelia, Elida, and Castula, took special delight in preparing for the occasion. No one had ever planned an event just for the women of the village.

They planned a simple menu of salad, crispy fried tortillas, guacamole, and refried beans. Fresh pineapple and "store-bought" cookies marked the event as special, as did the prettily arranged plates and service.

With white paper covering the tables, a thick bed of pine needles on the ground, and palm leaves and flowers decorating the posts and tables, we had a lovely meeting space. In addition, one could look through the chicken-wire walls and beyond the plaza to the surrounding mountains and bright blue sky. It had a simple elegance no hotel could provide.

The great day dawned. Some of the staff finished the decorating while the rest whipped everything together in the kitchen. The village children were peeking in doors and windows and through the chicken-wire walls. They watched and giggled and scooted back home to report the goings-on to their mothers and then scurried back again to do more spying until the teachers hustled them into the school.

The hour arrived but not our guests. All the women of the village had been invited. Ten minutes after the hour, fifteen minutes after the hour, twenty minutes after the hour—no one! Then twenty-five minutes after the hour the women began to stream into the plaza from every direction, as if someone had given a signal.

They came dressed in their finest clothes. Even shabby dresses had been cleaned, pressed (with a heated flatiron filled with hot coals), and covered with a pretty apron.

Men were also showing up at the plaza and some were moving toward the door to watch, but they were shooed away. We were determined the women should have the opportunity to talk very frankly with one another without the inhibition of eavesdropping men.

The program opened with the singing of a few songs the women had learned at the consult. The visiting leadership team introduced themselves and provided some background information on the program. Then they requested that each of the village women give her name, age, number of children, number of years she had gone to school, and any other information she would like to share. It was clearly difficult for many of the women to speak in a large group, but with the men removed from the scene, they managed to do it. They did not object to the questions. In a society where the elders are honored and respected for their accumulated wisdom, people don't mind saying how old they are. As the day went on, the team up front told stories of great women—for example, religious leaders— and stories of women in other projects. The guided conversations moved step-by-step to a deeper level with increasing openness and participation. The women began to share thoughts and feelings with each other in a new way. They talked about their babies dying, about husbands who got mean when they drank, or about the struggle of being alone with the children for three months every year during the dry season when their husbands couldn't plant or find work in the area and had to go to work on one of the coastal plantations.

They also began to share their dreams. One girl stated her desire to be a nurse. An older woman said that she would like to be able to write her own name before she died. That seemed to serve as a release for other women, a number of whom said that they too wanted to learn how to read and write. Others opened up, and the event climaxed with a flood of ideas, emotions, and sharing of dreams.

For me, the finest moment came at the end of the closing conversation. A woman about forty years old stood up and spoke. She said that all of her life she had been afraid to stand up in a group and say what she thought but that she would never be afraid again. (She was as good as her word. She became one of the leaders in the community.) The same women who had arrived quietly, with varying degrees of nervousness and probably a little suspicion, left with smiles and were chattering away.

The ultimate demonstration of courage and strength in the village women was in their ability to endure. They survived pregnancies, poverty, water hauling, long treks to the river to scrub their clothes, street sweeping, house building, endless tortilla making, dying babies, and intestinal parasites—all with an enduring grace.

It seemed to me that the women in the community were quicker than the men to engage in the work of the project even though they had less free time. Maybe they were so used to dividing their time into compartments and spreading it around that it was less difficult for them to add one more thing. In any event, they were certainly a powerful force in Conacaste.

Side by Side

A special program is offered during winter break at De-Pauw University in Greencastle, Indiana. It gives students some rather exotic opportunities to undertake research, study, and/or social service—often in projects which send them to Third World countries—for course credit. In January 1980, Conacaste became one of those exotic offerings. An ICA staff member in the U.S. worked with Chaplain Fred Lamar at the university to create a program that could both further the education of the students and contribute to the Conacaste development project. In addition the chaplain wanted the students to have the firsthand experience of living in poverty so that they might be inclined to take up service work among the world's poor.

But what would be meaningful and of long-lasting value? What could students and residents work on together to the benefit of both? What was the most urgent need of the village at the moment? The answer to that was easy. They needed water—pure, clean water.

Conacaste had electricity by then, and clean, readily available drinking water was the second big dream of the village. Making that dream come true seemed completely beyond the capacity of the village. Conversations with anyone who knew something about water systems quickly gave us a clear idea of what had to be done and what problems would be involved to make water run from the faucets in Conacaste. We needed help from outside, lots of it. The events which combined to provide that help still amaze me.

Drinking water and water for irrigation presented different problems. A mountain stood between Conacaste and the river three kilometers away; high enough so that from the top, gravity would feed an irrigation system, but too low to reach the highest homes in the village. Moreover, bringing in potable water from the river could not be justified by potential economic returns. Experts recommended one deep well, which would pump water into a big reservoir at the high point of the mountain just above and behind the village. Water could be pumped up to this reservoir once a day and treated with chlorine as necessary. From that height it would come down with plenty of pressure to flow from taps anywhere in town. So the first step was to carve a big reservoir out of the stony ground. After that we could work on the well and delivery system. The DePauw construction team could help build the reservoir.

As the plan evolved, DePauw decided to send two teams. In addition to the construction team there would be a medical team to work on health problems in the area. The team would include a dentist, a doctor, a nurse, and six or seven premed or predental students. Each of the two teams, construction and medical, would provide its own supplies and equipment. Money would be sent for the purchase of basic necessities, if they were items that were abundant and inexpensive in Guatemala. Other things would be brought from the States. Conacaste citizens and project staff would be responsible for providing housing and meals and meeting other needs of the forty team members, including organizing transportation, purchasing tools and supplies, and arranging R & R on the weekends.

In order to house the students, we decided to construct a new building, which would subsequently become the first structure in Conacaste's planned industrial park. Construction materials donated by four Guatemalan companies were stacked up at the site. Soon staff and villagers were leveling ground, mixing cement, laying a brick floor, putting up steel girders and cement-block walls, and mounting a sheet-metal roof. Everyone worked hard to be ready for the "guest workers." On the night before the students were to arrive, lights were strung from a nearby house, and the construction went on until two o'clock in the morning.

My assignment was to meet the students at the airport with two chartered buses. That gave me a glimpse of cultural differences and attitudes regarding time. Our planeload of volunteers was three hours late because of weather conditions in Miami. I was on the edge of hysteria because I was sure the bus drivers were going to be upset, or maybe refuse to wait, or at the very least demand more money. I could see myself standing in the airport telling forty exhausted travelers I had no way to get them to the village and no place for them to sleep. I later realized that my anxiety was based on attitudes about time that the Guatemalans did not share. *"No hay problema"* (no problem), the bus drivers kept reassuring me. They visited with each other, had something to eat, took a little siesta, and shrugged off the delay as unimportant. Contrary to asking for more money or complaining, they were patient and helpful when it finally came time to load the mountains of luggage and equipment onto their buses. My anxieties were allayed by the bus drivers' relaxed attitudes so that I was ready for the forty team members when they poured into the luggage area in a stream of white nylon jackets.

Had the customs officers decided to open and inspect everything, we might have been at the airport the rest of the night. Fortunately, the National Committee of Reconstruction had given them papers of inventory and permission. The officers knew about the project, so the teams whisked quickly through the formalities. Although it was a tight fit, everyone and everything somehow made it onto the two buses, and we were off to Conacaste. We had begun the first of many DePauw/ICA joint projects.

The team spent the first week in Conacaste providing health care services and learning about the people. Some things surprised them, such as the fact that even poor villagers have their share of psychosomatic illness. The doctor laughed at his preconceived notions that psychosomatic illness was restricted to upper-class, educated people. The dentist pulled five hundred teeth. He bemoaned the fact that he couldn't give treatment instead, but the teeth were too far gone from lack of care. One old man had every tooth pulled. The dentist was appalled, but the patient was relieved and grateful. The medical team confirmed what those of us who lived in Conacaste already believed: the community's greatest health care needs were for preventive medicine and health education.

The second week the medical team—along with their sleeping bags—was loaded into the back of a big, open truck and sent off for several days to visit three remote and isolated communities. The people they encountered in these villages, scattered through an inhospitable countryside, had to walk miles and miles to meet basic needs—to get to a clinic or to the highway for a bus to the city. Supplies were occasionally brought in by trucks, though as often as not, they came by pack trains of burros or on people's backs. When the team returned to Conacaste, they were visibly shaken and vividly aware of the differences made by the presence of a human development project. These poor villages contrasted dramatically with Conacaste, where women were running preschools, adults

94

were attending literacy classes at night, electricity had been introduced, and meetings and work groups were focused on water, health, and agricultural projects.

They noted the hope that infused the Conacastans in contrast to the sense of hopelessness in the other villages, where the feeling of being able to create a better future for themselves was nonexistent. They experienced the thrill of saving a baby's life and the despair of watching another die. Since infant mortality in poor Latin American communities can be directly tied to the lack of pure drinking water, the value of the work the construction team was doing could not have been more dramatically demonstrated.

Meanwhile, the construction team was becoming the tiredest, "achingest" bunch of humans imaginable. At the end of the very first day, a strong, athletic young man described his humiliation:

> I thought I was doing terrific, especially out in that hot sun. I figure I'm in pretty good shape because I play in sports and work out regularly and all that. I was moving pretty fast for a long time. But finally I knew I had to take a break or I was going to die! I flopped down on the ground and I looked at this scrawny little old man who was at least sixty years old. He was just working—digging, hauling, swinging that pick and using that shovel—as steady as when we started. So after a while I hauled myself back off the ground, and he was still going. I never did see him rest, at least not for more than a couple of minutes leaning on his shovel. I thought I was pretty strong, but that guy was something! Even the women just went on and on, hauling the dirt and all.

Every morning the construction team was up on the mountainside. Thirty students and faculty advisors were joined by at least that many villagers. Any ICA staff not assigned to medical or kitchen duty worked on the reservoir project as well.

The mountain sloped so steeply that we hired a grader to scrape out an access road. But after that first day, the work was done by hand. Day by day the reservoir was carved out of the stony ground until there was a twelve-foot square hole at the top, twelve- to fourteen-feet deep in the center. As the crew went deeper into the ground it was necessary to create wooden ramps so that wheelbarrows could be filled with dirt below, pushed up the steep incline, and then dumped out away from the construction. Of course, that became an increasingly difficult job. Big stones had to be hauled up by hand. All this was done in the blazing sun, where the temperature sometimes rose to over 100 degrees Fahrenheit. The desert conditions made the sweat dry fast, increasing the danger of dehydration, which made it imperative to keep a good supply of water and soft drinks on site.

Even when the hole had been dug to the proper size and proportions, the job was still a long way from being done. Next, the team had to line the hole with steel mesh to hold the cement. The cement had to be mixed by hand on flattened areas of ground and then hauled down in the wheelbarrows or lowered in buckets. The villagers were experts at mixing the sand, cement, and water with hoes into just the right consistency.

After the hole was lined with cement, we had to build an edge wall of cement blocks to rim the top, then coat the reservoir with a special black sealer similar to the tar used on flat roofs but of a special chemical composition so it would not poison the water. It was a slow, painful process. But what a thrill for everyone to finally look at the completed task. We had finished a mammoth job in an incredibly short period of time through determination and teamwork. We had taken our first giant step toward clean water.

What did we have after the two weeks of constant labor that followed the arrival of the DePauw team? Obviously, we had a huge, cement-coated, water-sealed hole in the ground up on the mountain. We also had a good-sized pile—so to speak—of rotten teeth that had been giving their owners a great deal of pain and discomfort. We had in addition diagnosed and treated many people's ailments and even saved a few lives. Some villagers had learned a little about how they could keep themselves in better health.

What was less obvious may have been more important. The individuals involved in the project were changed in significant and subtle ways. We had started off with two sets of people—the villagers and the visitors—observing and taking stock of each other, even competing a little. At the end of two weeks, both team members and villagers had new friends and interests and had experienced a great deal of pride in the job they had done together. I don't believe the villagers thought anyone had come in and done something for them or to them but rather that friends had given them a helping hand, a big difference from a do-gooder handout. And I think ICA can take credit for planting that concept in the minds of the villagers. Over and over from the earliest conversations, even before the project began, ICA kept saying, "You have to decide it, plan it, and do it. This is no giveaway program—in the end it is up to you." The students on the other hand had witnessed people pitching in and working alongside them rather than being passive recipients of their aid.

Perhaps the forty students were the biggest beneficiaries. We had a formal conversation with them on their last evening in Conacaste. They had some deeply moving and telling statements to make about their experience, many expressing—in their own ways—a determination to re-think the direction of their lives.

I especially remember one young man who said he had thought that most of the world lived the way he did and that poverty was the exception. Intellectually speaking, he knew that most of the world's population came from the rural areas and were poor, but that did not have meaning for him until he found himself in the reality of a poor village. Now he had come to understand that his comfortable life was, in fact, the exception in the world. He recognized that it was a difficult fact to face but added that it had made him very aware of both his good fortune in having such an excellent education and his responsibility for using that education well. He said he needed to reexamine how he could best use that gift to better serve humanity.

A young woman said she had often thought that maybe poor people were lazy or not very bright. For her it had been a revelation to see firsthand how hard poor people had to work to stay alive. And she had discovered for herself the wisdom of the villagers, though it came from people who were short on book learning.

The Iowa Story—
Part I

A reservoir on the mountaintop did not an entire water system make. Since there was no sparkling spring bubbling up to fill the tank, a well was needed. There were no fancy trench-digging machines and cranes to lay down miles of water pipe for a delivery system. Instead, hours of backbreaking hand labor were required. And there were no faucets around town to control water usage once we had it. In other words, there was still a great deal of work to do before anyone was going to walk down to the corner to fill up a jug with pure, cool water.

For weeks on end villagers and staff alike dug trenches and laid plastic pipe donated by government and private agencies. Teams were organized by sectors, and special work days were periodically designated to keep things moving. ICA had instituted these special work days to mobilize the resources to get a particularly big task done and give us a leap forward on a long-term job. A work day might be all day or just a half-day, but it was a carefully planned, well orchestrated method of using the skills of a group of people effectively and getting them deeply engaged in the work of the project. In Conacaste we sometimes had work days involving only our staff; more often we invited the whole community to participate. A couple of people would be assigned to plan the day, delineating the individual tasks to be done, the number of people needed for each task, and an approximate time line. For instance, if we had a construction job, assignments might be as follows: ten people to dig with shovels and spades, one driver for the truck to get sand, six men on the truck to load sand, three people to mix cement, one person in charge of tools, four people to provide the crew with liquid refreshment and prepare lunch, and so on. If one task was likely to be short term, that team would have a backup assignment so it could automatically move on. Age, skills, and physical limitations were taken into consideration by those doing the assigning. Work days were generally enjoyable and fostered team spirit. Everyone could participate and make a contribution. At the close of the work day we would celebrate with a meal or refreshments and conversation. On major jobs, like the water system, work days were important in keeping spirits up. This kind of immediate, tangible progress kept the vision of the water system a reality.

While we as a community could do most jobs ourselves, there were a few things that had to be done by paid professionals. Conversations with a topnotch well-drilling company in Guatemala City had been discouraging. We could see no way to raise the money to meet their prices. Consequently, Conacaste spent a month on a waiting list for the services of the one and only government well-drilling rig and crew. But finally, notice came that Conacaste was next in line.

Meanwhile, a friend in Iowa had found three different well drillers who were willing to take trips to Conacaste at their own expense to help us in whatever way they could. They gave both technical advice and an expensive drill bit for use on the Guatemalan rig. When the Guatemala/U.S.A. crew hit water at one hundred feet, the North Americans advised stopping there, as it was adequate water (though just barely), and they felt there wasn't a very good chance of doing better. If we drilled deeper, there was a danger of losing the water altogether. The Guatemalan drilling crew decided to gamble on the chance for a greater output. Unfortunately, they lost the gamble—and the water. So we were back to square one.

In addition to working directly on the well, Americans, including a water engineer from the Iowa State Health Department, were assisting in other aspects of the water project. They worked with us on the design of the system and advised us on how we could purify the water. They helped us decide exactly where to locate each of the five water stations in town and how to create a design that assured efficiency, convenience, and good drainage. Each of the five sectors in town was to have a station with six or seven faucets. No one in town would have to walk more than two blocks to get water—preferably so that any uphill climb would be with "empties."

The Iowa volunteers worked out the basic design and explained how it would function. They said they would search for donations of pipes, fittings, and faucets for the stations and ship them to us with the design and with the pieces numbered. Then one of the men looked at me and said, "Donnamarie, you can explain it to the villagers—it will be something like 'paint by number.'" I said to myself, "Oh sure, why not?" It was a little hard to picture myself doing plumbing and construction by following a number code and then explaining it to grown men in my bad Spanish, but I was willing to try almost anything for the sake of running water.

The volunteers were very helpful, but it soon became clear that for one of them this experience had turned into more than an opportunity to provide some technical assistance to the people of a Guatemalan village. Buck White had been deeply moved by his short stay in Conacaste. Buck owned a well-drilling company in Iowa. I guess he was typical of the well-fed, comfortable American. He was also a church-going man. He even taught an adult Sunday school class. He and his wife and children were active participants in the life of their small town church in Gladbrook, Iowa. Generally, one can safely assume that people who spend a great deal of their own money to live in what, for them, are very uncomfortable situations in order to help others, must be compassionate human beings—as Buck obviously was. And when compassionate human beings are set down in the midst of suffering, they frequently feel great pain themselves. Buck was clearly feeling the pain of being in Conacaste. Through an experience I personally (and inadvertently) led Buck into, that pain was intensified. It is also probably safe to say that one of the most remarkable episodes in the Conacaste story grew out of that experience.

Buck wanted to get some good pictures of Conacaste, so I agreed to take him to the highest spot above the village where he would have a nice view. We took the long, easy way up, past the reservoir, then across a cornfield (the vertical type—which was a shock the Iowans never did get over)—and on up the steep back side of the peak over the village. At the top there is a breathtaking view, and Buck took many pictures. Then I suggested we take the fast way back, straight over the edge, weaving our way down through the yards of all the little houses of the poor clinging tenaciously to the side of the mountain. It was not too difficult a walk, and I thought he would be interested in seeing some of the homes, and I knew that the people would be pleased to meet him. All was going very well until we stumbled into the yard of a woman I had forgotten about. She was retarded and had had several babies she wasn't really capable of caring for, even in the most basic way. There at our feet was a baby lying in the dirt, naked and scrawny, covered with feces, snot, and flies. That child was the saddest, most sickening sight I have ever seen. I was nauseated even though I had been somewhat hardened by prior experience. It was not the kind of thing one gets used to.

Buck, however, was in a state of shock. The rest of the way down the hill he kept asking rapid-fire questions: "How can you stay here? How can you do without meat? Can you really help these people? Why are you doing this?" He declared that those of us who lived in the project were saints and that he would tell his Sunday school class about our work. He also said he would mobilize his community to help us. We knew Buck was sincere, but frankly, we didn't count on a great deal of help from his friends in Iowa. We had learned from experience how easy it is to slip back into comfortable, old patterns and forget the experience of another kind of life a thousand miles away.

Actually, we had a good time with Buck, but the best time was one day at lunch, which was always served buffet style. Whoever was assigned to lunch preparation would see that it was set out by 12:15. People could wander in as they finished their work. Buck had not been exactly ecstatic over our food; it lacked variety and meat, and he found the desserts a little spartan. One day, those of us who were already seated and eating were more than a little surprised to hear Buck give a great big, happy "ahhhh" as he served himself from the buffet. We were even more surprised to see him sit down with two plates, one of which was heaped with a creamy pile of refried beans. He had not previously shown much interest in beans, but we liked them very much, especially the kind we were having that day. Kellogg Company had donated cases of instant beans (like instant potatoes). They were tasty and a great timesaver. We sauteed onion in margarine and mixed it into the powdered beans with water and heated them. I had never seen them sold in the States, so I was surprised Buck even knew about them. He ate everything on the first plate, set it aside, and with a smile pulled the plate of beans before him. Then he took a large mouthful, looked horrified, and gagged. I have never seen greater disappointment on anyone's face. "I thought it was chocolate pudding!" he said.

When the time finally came for Buck and the others to leave, we expressed our appreciation and our sorrow at seeing them go. For their part, they vowed to search for people willing to donate the materials we needed for the water stations. Despite our reservations, we saw them off with hopeful hearts.

Everyone labored on—digging trenches and laying pipe. We had decided where to put the water stations; we just needed our materials and instructions. So we waited— and waited—and waited. Finally we telephoned Iowa. The economy was bad, they said, and it was hard to find donors, but they'd get them. And so we waited some more.

As Buck later explained, the turning point came when he was sitting in church one Sunday. The minister's sermon that day was about how people often have good intentions that they neglect to fulfill. I don't know the details, but Buck said he was suddenly filled with guilt thinking about the promise he'd made to the Conacaste Project. At the end of the service, he jumped up determined to do something about it. That very day began the organization of an extraordinary set of events in Iowa.

After some conversations and meetings, Buck and some of his church friends decided to send a team to Conacaste. They would bring with them the materials and tools necessary to do the planned work. Not only would they help construct the water stations, they would also build playground equipment for the children and provide fabric and sewing classes for the women. In addition they decided to open participation in their project to people outside their own church. Those who went to Conacaste would be required to cover their own transportation and a share of the food costs. Money was to be raised to put in the new well and provide the pump and transformer for it. By the time the group was ready to leave for Guatemala, the project had been written up in Iowa newspapers and been the subject of radio and television broadcasts. Money came in from all directions—from individuals, other churches, social agencies, and businesses. The quantity and value of contributed tools and building materials that piled up was astonishing. Some people were so determined to go to Guatemala they took out second mortgages on their homes. Homemakers took part-time jobs. One woman took out a loan, knowing she would have to get a job to pay it off when she returned.

In Conacaste the excitement began to match that of Iowa. We compiled "shopping lists," wrote and received a flurry of letters, practically lived on the phone, and busily dug up streets for the pipes like a bunch of moles. The Iowa group was to arrive on the weekend after Thanksgiving and planned to be in Guatemala for two weeks.

The Iowa Story had begun. A chain reaction had been set off that would surprise us all.

Our Eastern "Angel"

*D*uring the time the Iowans were preparing for their foray into human development, I returned to the Institute of Cultural Affairs in Chicago to take eight weeks of courses known as The Global Academy, a highly disciplined, intensive set of university-level studies. I was also making the necessary preparations for my wedding to George West, whose position as director of the project would keep him in Guatemala until the wedding. We had decided to be married in Chicago so that more of our friends and family could attend. I was to finish at the academy by Thanksgiving, see the Iowans off to Guatemala, and complete the wedding preparations. The Iowans would return two weeks later, George would arrive in Chicago a week after that, and the wedding would take place on December 21. It was assumed that while I was in Chicago I would help the Iowans out if they ran into any snags.

Phone calls from Buck White and Dick Marks, a

longtime ICA associate from Iowa who was helping organize the trip, were pulling me out of classes and out of bed with increasing frequency as the time drew nearer for the group to leave. To top it off, there had been hints that a ticket might be donated for me to go along. It was a possibility that both thrilled and terrified me since that would leave only one week to prepare for the wedding when we returned to Chicago. Still, I wanted desperately to participate in the Iowa/Conacaste effort.

In Iowa things had been moving rapidly. A mountain of donated goods had accumulated,which the volunteers were busily packing. The plan was that all twenty-seven people, after celebrating Thanksgiving in Iowa, would drive to Chicago (in camper trucks and a pickup), stay one night at ICA, and leave from O'Hare Airport the next morning on Eastern Airlines. ICA staff would host the group at a dinner where the newcomers could be given information regarding the history and work of the organization. The Iowa guests could get a good night's sleep in the ICA Conference Center rooms. Everything was falling into place.

Then the bomb dropped. The Saturday before they were to leave, I received a frantic phone call from Buck White in Iowa. Among the materials they were bringing were a giant spool of electrical line, pipes and fittings, tools, two submersible pumps, and a huge electric transformer, constituting literally tons of stuff. And until that moment no one had realized that there was no way to pay for the transport of the materials. That mountain of goods was *in addition* to the luggage for all the people.

We were in a situation right out of *Catch-22.* If the volunteers used their money for the well drilling to ship the equipment, there wouldn't be any money left to drill the well. If they saved their money and went without their tools and materials, they wouldn't be able to do anything with the hole once they had drilled it. If they sent the materials and stayed home, it still wouldn't work because the villagers and ICA staff didn't have the skills to do the job.

I could hardly believe what Buck White said to me on the phone. "Donnamarie, we are counting on you to convince Eastern Airlines to take this stuff for us, free. We know you can do it!" It sure was great that they knew I could do it because I sure didn't. To make matters worse, I realized that with Thanksgiving coming there was only Monday, Tuesday, and part of Wednesday to find the right person at Eastern.

I tried hard to sit quietly and think. I didn't know a soul at the airline, at any level. After many phone calls and a lot of running around, I determined that I didn't even know anyone who knew anyone at Eastern. To add to my gloom, various people kept assuring me that the airlines never made any exceptions or did any special favors.

By Monday noon I was in a state of near terror. Drastic action was required. The only thing I could think of was to reach into a grab bag of Eastern employees and rummage around until I found the right executive. Mr. or Ms. "Right" was the person with sufficient compassion, caring, guts, and power to put that equipment on a plane and get it to Guatemala.

Where to begin? I decided to call the reservations office in downtown Chicago and ask a clerk for help. My story to the woman who answered the phone was simple: "I need to talk to someone at Eastern who has some clout. I have a real emergency regarding movement of materials with a large group of people who are flying to Guatemala next Saturday on Eastern." She couldn't have been nicer or more helpful. She got the handbook with the names of executives in the office in Oak Brook and started reading through the list. We discarded some of the names because their job titles were too remote from the situation to be useful. The final target I selected was Mr. Toby (A.W.) Jones, Passenger Sales. He was to be my victim. I was determined that if he wasn't the right person to do the job, I had to convince him to lead me to the right person. At that point I didn't care if I had to weep and plead my way through the whole Eastern executive staff.

It took a few hours to make contact, but by late Monday afternoon I had the gentleman on the phone to ask for an appointment. He was most agreeable and was willing to see me, but he couldn't figure out when. He was tied up for the rest of that day, would be in a meeting starting at nine on Tuesday morning, and wouldn't be in the office at all on Wednesday. I told him that I always got up very early in the morning and asked how early he started work. He said that he was an early riser and that if I was willing to get to his office by 7:30 the next morning, he would see me. That meant leaving before six to allow for the morning traffic. But then, I would have been willing to meet him in the middle of Lake Michigan at four o'clock in the morning if necessary.

Twenty minutes before the appointed hour I was sitting in my car in the parking lot of the Eastern offices with an adrenalin level that surely must have made medical history. If Eastern didn't agree to help us somehow, I couldn't begin to imagine what we would do.

Toby Jones was just as pleasant in person as he had been on the phone. We settled down with our coffee, and I filled him in on the project, the work of ICA, the work with the DePauw students, and finally the story of what the people in Iowa were doing and our terrible dilemma. Mr. Jones grasped the implications immediately and began to think it through out loud: "That is impossible, but we must find a way to do it; their work will be for nothing otherwise. I can't think how we can do it, but there must be some way. We can't send the things by freight because they would arrive too late. The only possibility is to send everything with them as luggage. That is no problem as far as Miami because it is a big plane, but from Miami to Guatemala we use only 727s. If there is a full plane, the luggage hold will be crammed. First let me call and find out if the plane is full." The plane was solidly booked, of course, that close to Christmas. The Ladinos who shop in the States pass through Guatemala, which serves as the changing point for all the Central American countries.

I sat there in despair, but Toby Jones turned to me and said, "We'll find a way to do it, somehow." He got on the phone and talked to people in Chicago and Miami. After many calls he said, "Okay, here's what we do. Everything must go with the people as luggage." (Doesn't everyone take transformers, pumps, and pipes on vacation with them?) He proceeded to give me careful instructions to relay to the volunteers in Iowa. There were precise, maximum measurements and weight requirements that could not be exceeded, or Eastern would be in trouble with the unions. Footlockers and duffel bags were the best containers. Check-in officials at O'Hare would give priority to the Iowans' "luggage" and count the pieces through. The transformer and reel of electrical line presented a separate problem because they were too large to pass through the opening into the luggage hold of the smaller plane. Those would go as far as Miami on the Eastern jet and then be sent by freight on a larger Pan Am plane to Guatemala. We had to pray they would arrive four or five days after the group. That was harder to control because they would be on a different airline.

There was no way to adequately thank Mr. Jones, but I said it in every way I could think of. Once the people in Iowa had their instructions, they had to buy additional footlockers and redistribute the weight, but it was feasible. The only freight charges would be for the transformers and the reel of wire from Miami to Guatemala City. And Toby Jones had a ticket for me, but I was not supposed to let George know in advance. I was to be a surprise package from Iowa.

When we arrived at the Eastern check-in counter that Saturday morning, we were given VIP treatment. The Eastern staff remained cool as they checked in a seemingly endless supply of what surely must have represented the weirdest array of luggage they had ever seen. Twenty-two footlockers, twenty duffel bags, luggage for twenty-eight people, the transformer, and a reel of electrical line passed through that counter. Each piece had a number label corresponding to a list which itemized what was in each container. If number eighteen should get lost, at least we would know exactly which items were missing. Eastern was not about to lose anything, however. I have never seen better care taken of a group of airline passengers and their luggage.

When we landed in Guatemala, the group insisted I be the last person off the plane, so we could surprise George. When I walked into the customs area, they were standing in a semicircle around George, watching his face. If he had been more alert, he might have noticed their odd behavior. I got about four feet from him before he saw me; then, what a smile!

The Iowa Story—
Part II

*T*he people from Iowa represented a wide variety of talents and professions. I can call to mind a realtor, farmers, an electrician, homemakers, a minister, a well driller, and educators. The age range extended from fourteen to eighty. It was the eighty-year-old who was the first one up in the morning, fixing coffee for everyone.

Whatever their age or background, they had a common goal. While the water system was the major target in everyone's mind, they had also created some side programs: a playground project and sewing classes. One of the men had designed a great jungle gym and brought it in pieces to Guatemala, where it was put together like a gigantic jigsaw puzzle. A couple of the men then erected a playground-size swing set in the plaza for the older children. After the Iowans left, I often saw adults on it, sitting side by side, swinging gently as they visited. Next, they constructed a solid teeter-totter beside the grade school where there was not sufficient space for other equipment.

All the play equipment was a miracle of design and construction and would be a source of pleasure for the village children (and adults) for years to come.

Two of the women came prepared to give sewing classes and arrived with yards and yards of donated fabrics, thread, pins and needles, and patterns of all kinds and sizes. Their enthusiasm, however, was destined to be put through something of a traumatic test. We had been adamant in our advance instructions that out of respect for the self-esteem of the villagers, nothing was to be given away free. Cloth, as I recall, was to be sold for ten cents a yard, and the women were required to work on their sewing project in the class. The sewing center was housed in the front classroom of the grade school, which was not in session at the time. One of our staff had been given the assignment of helping the Iowa women set up and introducing them to the community. Then that staff member had to move on to help some of the other volunteers with their communication problems. There weren't many of us with adequate bilingual skills, but except for one fluent, Colombian-born bilingual in the Iowa group, the responsibility for communication was mostly up to our staff. Consequently, we kept moving around the village, trying to be of help wherever it was most needed at a given moment.

I was walking down the road near the school when one of the sewing instructors came running after me, calling for help. She looked close to tears. We hurried into the school, and it didn't take me a fraction of a second to understand why she was upset. If you have ever had the misfortune to be present at a major annual sale in a famous women's clothing store or fabric department, you may have some idea of the chaos. The Conacaste women were being offered the bargain of the century. It was even hard for me to look at those piles of pretty fabrics at ten cents a yard and not react with bargain-hunter instinct, so what could be expected from people who had always lived in poverty? The women from Iowa weren't going to control that situation with mere sign language.

But that was not the only problem the supervisors of the sewing center faced. They also had to deal with the fact that the classes included expert seamstresses, women who barely knew what a needle was, and, of course, every level between. In addition, we had to watch out for people who wanted to buy the fabrics at our bargain prices simply to take them elsewhere to sell for a profit. Our instructors had to have some help from us, but eventually the sewing center calmed down, sorted itself out, and offered valuable service to the community.

Meanwhile, the major job of building the water system was moving forward. A small team of men worked their way through the sectors, constructing a water station in each, with a few of the local sector men helping them. It was not a quick or easy job, and it required a lot of plumbing and cement work. A pretty, blue ceramic tile was embedded in the cement at each station as a finishing touch. On the tile was the project symbol of the Conacaste tree and the inauguration date of the water system. Conacaste is the name of a tree of beautiful and strong wood. The community had selected the tree as their symbol, and their slogan was "the people of good wood." A stylized drawing of the tree was used as the logo on the project brochure and letterhead. The Iowans copied the design onto the tiles as their gift signature.

As the water stations were completed, each sector was finishing up the pipe laying and hookup. The sectors were doing whatever was necessary for their water connection with the exception of Sector I, where the people had been somewhat lazy and uncooperative during the long ditch-digging period. For reasons we never did understand, the people in that section of Conacaste were prone to finagling someone else to do their work for them. They seemed to believe that the project staff and the people from Iowa were going to stop what they were doing, dig the last fifty feet of ditch for them, and install their pipes. Every day or two one of our staff would remind them that they might want to get started on that stretch if they expected to have a water station, but no action was forthcoming. Finally, the day came when a staff member went to them and said, "The water station in Sector IV will be completed by tonight. If Sector I is not ready in the morning, you will not have a water station. No one else is going to do it for you. If in the future you want to be added on to the system, you will have to pay for it, build your own station, and convince the rest of the town to do without water while you hook up. You will have to decide." It didn't take them long. By noon the men out working on that street were packed so close together, they had to be careful not to whack each other with their picks and shovels. They dug furiously, and they got their water station.

While that activity was going on, Buck White and his colleagues had been negotiating with the well-drilling company, DAHO POZO. They had obtained an excellent price and had the company's multimillion-dollar rig in Conacaste carving out a well. That remarkable machine dug into the ground like a spoon into soft butter and with remarkable speed. The owners of the drill had even agreed to dig a second well for us, on credit, at the demonstration farm. They were so impressed by what the Iowans were doing for Guatemala and by what Eastern Airlines had done for the Iowans (and for Guatemala), how could they say no?

At the same time, there were discussions with INDE, the national electric company. They were critical of the water project because an extension electrical line had to be run out to the well area, the transformer put in place, and all of it connected to the new well. If you will remember, in our previous work with INDE, it had taken a year to get electricity in the village and another six months to get the meters. It was unnerving to think how fast we needed action now. But we weren't taking into account the chain reaction of miracles that had been set off. Each act of unselfish generosity had generated the next. The Iowans had been impressed by the work of ICA and the villagers; Eastern Airlines was impressed by the Iowa group; DAHO POZO was impressed by the Americans and by what Eastern had done; and INDE was impressed by them all! At the end of the two-week Iowa visit we pumped water up into the big tank, and we were ready to turn on the faucets. Of all the celebrations I remember during my nearly six years in the project, I think the one with our friends from Iowa was perhaps the most moving and beautiful. I have always felt sorry that the DePauw team couldn't be there to share in that event.

The big celebration was to be held in the evening. During that day each sector decorated its water station, cutting and dragging in huge branches of palms and tying them into lovely arches. They fastened flowers into the palms and made chains and bouquets. Each sector tried to outdo the others. The sectors selected a spokesperson and a *madrina*, something like a beauty queen or princess, though chosen for popularity rather than appearance.

As darkness fell, the crowds began to gather in the plaza. Our master of ceremonies was one of the villagers from the project staff. He had developed a great flair and style for the role of MC. Men came forth with blazing torches held high. The five madrinas stepped out in long, colorful dresses and flowers in their hair, leading the procession to the first water station. There must have been several hundred excited people in the procession, not the least of whom were the Iowans. The procession gathered people and excitement as it moved through the town. At each water station the sector representative gave a speech, an Iowan responded with a few words, the celebrants sang a song, the madrina christened the water station, and the water was turned on.

It would be impossible to capture the emotion of that evening. I saw tears stream down the faces of both

Guatemalans and foreigners. There was a profound sense of brotherhood, joy, and victory. So many people had been involved in the creation of this great moment. I vividly recall the minister from Iowa, walking in front of me at one point, shaking his head from side to side and saying over and over, "There has never been such a time."

After all five stations had been formally inaugurated, the procession moved back to the plaza for a night of refreshments and dancing to the music of the marimba band. I don't think there is any happier music than that of the marimba. It is the symbol of celebration to Guatemalans.

So with overflowing hearts and exhausted bodies, we collapsed onto the plane to return to the States for the celebration of Christmas. For me, there was also finally time to begin preparing for our wedding. It was a glorious season.

Give Them the Seed

Close behind electricity and drinking water in the priorities established in the community plan came irrigation for the croplands. Subsistence farming was the economic base in Conacaste. Most of the families in the village owned a small piece of land and survived by farming the life out of it. Not only was the originally rich volcanic soil wearing out, it was being used to feed more and more people. The parcels of land were carved into ever smaller parcelas as each generation in the family was given a share.

Electricity and pure drinking water were certainly keys to improving the quality of life in Conacaste, but more was needed. The disfranchised had to be brought into the mainstream of contemporary life. On the one hand, they had to have self-confidence and a belief in their own ability to direct their future. On the other, they needed the tools and techniques of a modern economy—seed, land, equipment, training—if they were to survive.

In a land that has fertile soil, an ideal temperature

119

range and, except for a long dry season, excellent agricultural conditions, the richest and best farmer in the community made a top annual income of only eight hundred dollars. Fairly prosperous families earned about five hundred dollars each year to take care of their needs. You can imagine what it was like for the poor. Each family saved from their crops the corn and beans they needed for survival and sold what was left for small amounts of cash. When the rains were too little, too late, or too much, they were in trouble. It took ninety days to get the corn in and out of the ground and sixty to ninety days to plant and harvest the beans, chilies, and tomatoes. For six or seven months of the year it didn't rain, so during the dry season a farmer couldn't plant unless he had irrigation.

A few farmers with wells on their land had a pump and some plastic tubing with which they practiced flood irrigation. They got quite good results, but it took large amounts of water, which meant a lot of money for gasoline to run the pumps. Also, there was always the possibility the well would run dry or collapse in an earthquake.

At the end of the consult I had gone back to the States to rent my house and wrap up business. Considering my background, I had expected to be assigned to work either in health or small business development when I returned to Conacaste. Instead, I was assigned to work on irrigation, something I knew absolutely nothing about. The man assigned to be my working partner, Don Richards, was about as knowledgeable as I was. We protested our ignorance of agricultural matters but to no avail. Our assignment was to research the various options in irrigation equipment and techniques, meet with the farmers to talk about the options, and set up a very small demonstration system on one farmer's parcela within three months. In addition, we had to talk some company into donating materials for the demonstration. Finally, we had to explain what we were doing to the farmers in our broken Spanish. If Don and I had taken ourselves too seriously, we might have been overwhelmed and given up. Fortunately, he had a good sense of humor and I had my boundless optimism. So we plunged ahead.

I soon learned more about irrigation systems than I had ever thought I wanted to know and began to develop a genuine interest in what could happen when irrigation was introduced into a dry land. After all, the Israelis had turned desert into lush gardens with it.

We learned there are three basic types of irrigation. First is the flood type, which means simply pumping water over the land via ditches. Second, there is the sprinkler type, which is heavily used in the States. As you drive by sprinkler-irrigated fields, you see long pipes stretching across the fields above the crops with evenly spaced sprinklers on top of the pipes. Like flood irrigation, it uses enormous quantities of water, plus much of the water evaporates as it whirls through the air. There are also limits on the time of day one may irrigate because of the danger of leaf burn from watering in a blazing sun.

The third kind—trickle, or drip, irrigation—seemed the best for Conacaste because it uses about half as much water. Narrow, flexible tubing lying directly on the ground snakes up and down the rows of the field. Every twenty-four to thirty inches there are little valves in the top of the tubing. Water drips or trickles out of each valve with an equal amount of pressure no matter how far it is from the water source. A pump keeps the water moving and is equipped with filters to extract debris that might clog the valves. The water goes directly to the base of the plants, rather than being sprinkled everywhere and encouraging weeds. Also, it is easy to add liquid fertilizers to the water in precisely measured amounts to feed every plant equally. What's more, it doesn't matter what hour of the day you water because the water and nutrients go straight to the roots.

When I first heard about drip irrigation, it sounded perfect for Guatemala. Don and I thought we had found the right answer—until the "experts" began to puncture holes in it. One after another, they told us it would be impossible for our uneducated villagers to manage the sophisticated equipment called for in drip irrigation. They explained how the filters had to be closely watched and cleaned regularly, fertilizers measured carefully by formula and added at the right time, and valves checked. We could see that it was more complicated than the other types of irrigation systems and gradually came to accept their assessment—which turned out to be wrong.

We did establish a demonstration project, however. One of the companies agreed to donate a pump, some pipe, and two sprinklers. A village farmer who had a well agreed to let us place the demonstration on a tiny plot of his land near the road in full view of all passersby. We came in ahead of schedule in setting up the demonstration, but what had we proved? Only that if someone gives you the equipment and you can scrape up the money for gasoline, plants will grow well with adequate water. We may have convinced a few farmers that they wanted an irrigation system, but we had not shown Conacaste an irrigation system that was really viable for its farmers.

The big breakthrough came when we met an Israeli engineer, Yigal Harpaz, who was working with the Inter-American Development Bank (IADB) in Guatemala. For two years he had been looking for the right place to demonstrate drip irrigation, which he believed was a superior method of irrigation for Guatemala. He claimed it was nonsense to say the farmers could not be trained to use the technology and use it well. What's more he offered to prove it. He had an Israeli friend, Moishe, working for the irrigation firm TOPKE. Moishe was an expert in drip irrigation. The two men came out to visit Conacaste and look over the farms, and thus began the long process of attaining drip irrigation and forming a farmers' cooperative capable of managing it.

We knew there would be a great deal of work to do,

but we had no idea how much. We were inundated with
questions: Where would the water come from? How could
an irrigation project be financed? How could it be managed? How could the farmers be adequately trained? In
development projects around the world, farmers had re-
peatedly gotten themselves into debt and lost the land
they used as collateral. When we were trying to set up the
loan from IADB, the National Committee of Reconstruction (CRN) constantly fussed at us for reassurance that the
Guatemalan farmers would be protected from that danger.

It was a big job with great potential. Yet, we had
thought so small. We had been ready to write up a proposal to IADB for a $50,000 sprinkle irrigation system.
Now our Israeli friends were urging us to submit a
$500,000 proposal for drip irrigation.

First of all we had to select and convince a farmer to
be the guinea pig to prove to IADB that our villagers were
equal to the challenge. After long discussions, Señor
Manuel Samayoa was chosen. He was one of the best
farmers in the village, he had a good, visible location for
placement of a demonstration system, and he was enthusiastic about trying out a new method. TOPKE was to loan
the equipment plus the expertise of Moishe and his helper,
who would provide Señor Samayoa with three months of
training. One half of one *manzana* (a piece of land slightly
larger than one acre) was to be used as the demonstration
plot. A crop of corn would be grown on one part in order
to measure production against the usual village yield. Another part was to be planted in snow peas, which was an
experiment at that altitude and temperature. A third part
was to be put into broccoli, which was a first-ever crop for
Guatemala.

For the first three months one of the TOPKE staff was
by Señor Samayoa's side almost daily. For the second three
months Señor Samayoa was on his own. At the end of the
six months the crop results exceeded our wildest expecta-
tions. In the midst of the dry season Señor Samayoa had

more than tripled the average corn yield. The snow peas had done moderately well in spite of the fact that the altitude was a little too low and the temperature a little high for them, and the broccoli was a great success. Señor Samayoa took a truck of broccoli directly to hotel and restaurant owners, who snatched it up and said they would gladly buy whatever he could produce. Señor Samayoa didn't need any further convincing in regard to drip irrigation.

Meanwhile, during all the planting, growing, harvesting, and selling, Yigal and Moishe were helping us write the proposal to IADB. In addition, the IADB man helped us get approval for the project from the Guatemalan government. TOPKE calculated the volume of water needed from the river, and the Guatemalan government conducted a feasibility study. The conclusion was that there was adequate water, even during the dry season, to use the river as our source.

However, bringing water from the river to Conacaste was not a simple matter. It meant constructing a pumping system and running pipelines under the highway, up over a mountain, three and a half kilometers down the other side, and finally, up into a reservoir on a slightly lower mountain. From the reservoir it could travel downhill by gravity to farms. It was no small undertaking.

But it was not only a question of money, design, construction, and training. Both IADB and the Guatemalan government wanted every conceivable safeguard built into the plan. We in the project were in total agreement with the requirement, but it was a tough job to figure out all the possible pitfalls that could occur and the ways to avoid them.

We began doing research on similar types of projects that had been unsuccessful and found they shared certain characteristics. Failure could be predicted where people

124

were allocated enough money for a first crop and for the purchase of irrigation equipment but were not provided with adequate training and support systems. Also, farmers needed to know something about money management and planning. "Planning" to them meant scraping up enough money for tomorrow or next week. They were not used to looking ahead, and it was unreasonable to expect them, without training, to set aside enough money from a crop to make payment on equipment and to save sufficient funds for the next crop, including a built-in contingency fund for possible disasters. It was clearly necessary to include in the plan, at the outset, the structures and procedures needed to protect the inexperienced farmer from failure.

Many people worked for months developing, writing, and revising the proposal, and when it was done, IADB, the government, and the ICA staff felt it had an excellent chance to succeed.

The basic components of the proposal were as follows:

1. The farmers using the irrigation system were required to join the Conacaste Agricultural Cooperative.
2. The cooperative would own the central irrigation system.
3. IADB would make a $500,000 loan for construction of the system.
4. Loans to the individual farmers would be used for equipment in the fields, connection to the central system, and start-up costs for the first crop.
5. Purchases of seed and fertilizer would be made through the cooperative.
6. Crops would be sold through the cooperative. Cash would go to the farmer only after deductions for loan repayment and the emergency fund. This was to be built up as a hedge against possible crop failures.

Repayment of the 1 percent loan to the cooperative for the central system was to be deferred for ten years. The most exciting aspect of the IADB funding was that the loans were going directly to the people rather than to the government. It was the first time ever. When loans are made through governments, even if they are scrupulously administered, the interest rates are too high for the villagers. In the case of the Conacaste loan, ICA staff was responsible for money management, training, and the setting up of administrative systems for the first couple of years, or until such time as the bank and ICA agreed the farmers were ready to take over.

The disappointing part of the agreement was that the bank would not allow one dime to go to ICA even though we were required to take on an enormous workload and full responsibility. We agreed to the conditions because the prospect of success in a project with so much potential was too tempting to pass up. Three years later when we totaled up our staff hours, we realized it had cost us more than $500,000 in staff time and operating expenses to implement the loan.

We did convince IADB to approve a grant to hire two experienced Guatemalans to help the farmers take the required steps to establish a legal cooperative and to do the bookkeeping. They would also train the farmers to operate the co-op. This was important, as no one on our staff knew anything about co-op formation and management. A third Guatemalan was hired on a part-time basis to conduct training in irrigation farming.

We soon realized that the irrigation project would give rise to a new set of issues and problems that would require attention. Thirty or so farms dramatically increasing their production would not be of much value to the community unless they diversified their crops. In addition to diversification they needed to develop a guaranteed market. If the farmers all showed up at the city market with huge amounts of the same gorgeous produce, it would only push the price down. We decided that in order to get answers to these questions, we would have to get into the farming business and conduct practical experimentation with new crops.

We were lucky to have two companies who were eager to bid on the community's irrigation system. They were both ready to lend us equipment to train the farmers and to stimulate interest in drip irrigation. Each would consider it a coup to be the first company to mount a successful demonstration. But we had to provide detailed specifications for the companies before they could make their bids. Since none of us were engineers, we had to search for professionals to guide us in writing specifications. We were fortunate to have the general manager of Miles Laboratory in Guatemala City, Ing. Sergio Barrientos, as one of our supporters. He held three different engineering degrees himself and had several engineers on his staff. They worked with us for many hours, polishing details and working out the hitches.

When the specifications were done, the required notice was put in the newspapers. Four companies came forth to request the specifications, and three submitted bids by the deadline date. We were able to eliminate one bid immediately, but the other two, those from Tecnica Hidraulica and TOPKE, were a different case. When we read them, we found ourselves in a dilemma. The Tecnica Hidraulica bid was somewhat lower than that of TOPKE. While both companies had lent us equipment and technical assistance, TOPKE had been there first and had been very generous and good to work with. However, TOPKE had lost two exceptionally fine technicians with whom we had been working closely. Since TOPKE's price was higher and since they had lost the two technicians, we decided to go with Tecnica, as the equipment seemed of equal quality. It was a tough decision to make because we felt very grateful to TOPKE for their previous help.

One of the important ancillary requirements in the

127

specifications was that the company winning the contract give Conacastans first chance at unskilled jobs. That had the advantage of bringing some of the money from the company right back to Conacaste. For a long time most of that labor consisted of digging ditches for pipelines. The pipes had to run the three and one-half kilometers from the river to the reservoir site. Then other pipes stretched out in opposite directions from the reservoir down the side of the road, branching off to various areas surrounding the village.

It was our good fortune that, just at that point, a North American volunteer, John Foss, joined us. John had some experience in construction work, so he could keep a finger on the pulse of progress. It was John who came in one day with a story that epitomized what we were working for in Conacaste. At the reservoir construction site he had observed three or four of the men from the Conacaste Agricultural Co-op watching the mixing and laying of cement and asking questions. The construction foreman had been ignoring their questions and had been generally rude. When Jose Farjardo, one of the villagers, stepped up and asked him whether the cement was exactly right for pouring, the foreman lost whatever patience he had and shouted, "Why don't you get out of here? You have no business being here. I work for ICA."

But Jose stood his ground and let the foreman have it: "You don't work for ICA; you work for me. *You* work for *us*! ICA could go away tomorrow, or next week, or next year. We farmers of Conacaste will be here working to pay for this system. We will pay for the irrigation. You work for us." When I heard that, I knew that even if the water never ran in those irrigation pipes, we had won.

But, of course, eventually the water did run in those pipes. The first three farmers to bring in crops with drip irrigation in the dry season had planted before the central system was completed. Their production was phenomenal and gave dramatic proof of the value of irrigation. As I recall, the yield in tomatoes was something like seven times the previous average. They hit it lucky at the market too. The first farmer grossed $7,000, the second farmer $9,000, and the third around $6,000. Talk about excitement in that village! And they could do two more crops yet that year. Even after deducting past and future expenses, they were left with more money than they had ever dreamed of having.

There were delays in completion of the central system because of design complications with the filters at the river. In spite of that, by 1986 there were eighty members of the Conacaste Agricultural Cooperative. Although they had just begun irrigation, the majority of the farmers had increased their net income to about $1,400 per crop, an extraordinary improvement in their economic situation.

The Neighborhood

*F*or the first two years of the project the village was the work base from which I made a few day trips each week into Guatemala City. By the third year my responsibilities had shifted to the development of funding sources and the nurturing of relationships with friends and supporters located in the city, where I now spent four or five days each week, with weekends in Conacaste. Since daily commuting was too time-consuming, I had to find a place to live in Guatemala City.

Our criteria in searching for housing were basic: first came cost, second convenience, and third, safety. I was married by now, but George was needed much of the time in the village, and I would have to spend a good bit of time alone in the city.

An abundance of housing for individuals and couples who need temporary homes is available because Guatemala City has a generous supply of large universities. It is possible to rent a room with optional services such as cleaning, change of bed linens, meals, and personal laundry hand-scrubbed by a maid. The guest houses in which these rooms are located range from downright grubby to luxurious.

The first place I rented was fine, but when it was necessary for me to be in the U.S. for two months, we couldn't continue paying rent and we lost it. The second place we had was also fine, but if we had given the landlady a broom, she would have been able to fly, she was so unpleasant. Number three was the magic number. Our room cost $75 a month, with meals available for a dollar each. It was in an attractive, stable, old-fashioned neighborhood. Where I lived in Evanston, Illinois, was no safer, nor was it as convenient or interesting.

We lived in Zone 1, the heart of the city, three blocks from the National Palace and Central Plaza. At least eight different bus lines provided service from within two blocks of our door. Our house was in the middle of the block. On the corners were the ice cream/hot dog place, the National Music Conservatory, a delightful, small park, and an ordinary private house.

As far as I have been able to determine, there are no such things as zoning laws in Guatemala City. It is not unusual to see an elegant private home, a shoe repair shop, a tailor, a slum shanty, a church, a restaurant, a gas station, a cement-block factory, a grocery store, another elegant home, and a funeral parlor lined up side by side. What's more, nobody seems to be the slightest concerned nor does it appear to have any consequence in terms of property values. Guatemalan neighborhoods, therefore, have great variety and tend to be quite interesting.

The feature I enjoyed most about the neighborhood was its liveliness; it was a scene of constant activity, drama, and entertainment. The music conservatory was one hub of activity. There was usually a cacophony of sound rolling out of it, both vocal and instrumental—piano, horns, marimbas, and drums. Music came from the little park on the corner across the street too—nervous students getting a last moment of practice before auditioning for various musical programs. There were flutes, guitars, and horns, singly and in groups. A diagonal walk cut across the park and circled around the bust of a hero. The bust was on a five-foot pedestal with a ring of flowering plants around the base, which in turn was circled by a black, wrought-iron fence. Considering the size of the park, there were a remarkable number of trees and benches (for the abundance of lovers who frequented it). One line of benches faced the street, where people sat while waiting for the bus or while having their shoes shined for twenty-five cents. The lights in the park were old-fashioned and charming. The grass struggled to survive since people stepped on it, slept on it (often all night), and picnicked on it. During the dry season it nearly died altogether, only to burst forth green once again after a couple of rains.

In many places in the world you can be fined for throwing your trash on the ground. In Guatemala I had the impression you were expected to do so as a means of providing jobs for trash-pickup men. Our small park received its share of trash, but we had a little, round, grouchy man, who worked diligently to keep it spruced up and clean.

Next to the conservatory was the ice cream store, then the barber shop, and next to that was a strange-looking business establishment. When I first saw it, I thought perhaps it was some kind of collection depot for recycling old newspapers. As were most businesses in the city, it was constructed like a garage with an overhead metal door that was pulled down and secured with a padlock through rings embedded in the cement. Inside there was a glass showcase/counter, nearly buried in papers, set back a couple of feet from the front opening. The case was crammed with stacks of paper. More paper was stacked everywhere—on the counter, beside the counter, behind the counter, on the floor, and stuffed into plastic bags. It looked like a gigantic wastebasket the size of a two-car garage.

Upon closer inspection one could see that, in addition to the stacks, there were two strange wire racks on each side of the front where bunches of papers were suspended by heavy metal clips, resembling clothespins. In the midst of this mess, constantly shuffling papers and rearranging stacks, was the owner, easily as disreputable-looking as his store.

For a long time I passed by with nothing more than a glance since the place didn't show signs of providing any kind of service or product that we needed. What finally stirred my curiosity was the growing awareness that there was continuous activity in that odd place and that most of the people patronizing it were young. So, finally, I wandered over to see what was going on. It turned out to be a store selling sheet music and song books. On one of the vertical racks was current rock and country music; on another, classical music. Some of the stacks of music appeared to be new, but much of it was secondhand, complete with tears, finger marks, and spots from spilled coffee. I should have guessed what the shop was since it was practically on the doorstep of the music conservatory.

Next to the music store was an apartment building. Then came Cafe Pastel, a tiny restaurant the size of a garage. It had a terrazzo floor, little round tables with pretty cloths, and a profusion of hanging plants. Its main attraction and temptation to the passerby was a glass showcase at the front that was filled with fresh-baked goods like pineapple upside-down cake, cookies, and chocolate cake.

After that came our house, painted a sunny yellow with a deep-set window, encased in black, wrought-iron grillwork, which was typical of Latin America. It was common to see babies or family pets perched on the window ledges, enjoying the sun and watching the activity in the street.

On the other side of our house was a funeral home that

operated twenty-four hours a day. My initial reaction to the idea of living next to a funeral home was negative, but I quickly changed my mind. In fact, it was a great asset since it provided excellent security. The front had an open arch and double doors to the office that were never closed. Therefore, the employees saw and heard everything going on in the street. Late at night was undoubtedly a very boring time for them, so the slightest sound outside had them jumping up to look. They knew the people in the neighborhood and could immediately spot any strangers. Consequently, residents in the block didn't have to worry much about anyone fooling around with their cars or motorcycles. And I knew that if I came in late at night alone and anyone bothered me, one yell would bring three or four men on the run to help me. Once, when we arrived home by taxi from the airport after a short absence, they all ran out to grin and wave, the first to welcome us home.

Another helpful feature of the funeral parlor was its public phone. We didn't have a phone installed in the house for months, and there are not many handy public phones in the city, so I used the one in the funeral parlor. It was, though, a little disconcerting to arrange a business appointment while staring into the waxen face of a total stranger laid out in a coffin.

In the village most of the coffins I had seen were crude, rough pine boxes, no bigger than necessary for the particular body. In the city the coffins were wood, but generally carved, stained dark, and highly polished. Sometimes they were rectangular but more often a long oval. Many of the funeral homes had showrooms with coffins stacked on racks to the ceiling. As with other businesses, they were quite often like garages with no front wall, so I had seen plenty of coffins. Death is not hidden away in Guatemala. In fact, the streets surrounding the hospitals are generally full of funeral parlors.

As I worked at my desk at the front window of our house, I saw the coffins coming and going. I had seen many pickup truck deliveries, but one day I became aware of another way of delivery. A big, second-class passenger bus parked in front of our door. Its sign read "Antigua," and there were passengers on it. Since we are not on that route and the terminal was nowhere near us, I was surprised at first—until I looked up. The top of the bus was loaded with coffins, at least thirty of them. But naturally, I thought, the town of Antigua is famous for its beautiful, hand-carved furniture, so why not coffins as well? The funeral parlor crew obviously couldn't keep a bus load of people waiting long, and they didn't. They flipped the coffins off as if they were matchsticks. In five minutes the bus was gone, and it looked as if the neighborhood were having a sidewalk sale on coffins.

Around the corner from the funeral home was a tailor, where you could have a suit made, socks darned, and buttons sewn on. Next door was a shoe repair shop where rubber heels sold for fifty cents and leather for a dollar. They were both little hole-in-the-wall shops, but across the street was a grocery store that was even smaller—I've seen bigger closets. It was dark, grim, and grubby, but it was a great source of fruits and vegetables at low prices. Tomatoes might be a penny apiece, for example, or mangoes, five cents. To get inside, it was usually necessary to crawl over a woman who sat on the doorstep with a pan of coals, cooking tortillas or tamales. The doorway was high, so a small wooden box served as a step. It was precarious, but inside there were huge baskets on the floor, full of produce brought in that day. Some days there was a fine selection, other days, not. At the next corner was a small general store, where you could get basic supplies, from toilet paper to canned goods and liquor.

Across the street from our house was a ten-foot-by-ten-foot store owned by a plump, grey-haired old woman who took a fancy to us. I had the impression she felt that having foreigners shop in her store gave it class. She must have been robbed at some point, or maybe she was just naturally fearful, because her modest store counter was protected by bars and screening, making it necessary for her to open a little screen door to serve the customer. I couldn't imagine its being much protection against a serious thief, though. For us it was a handy place to buy a few eggs, a Coke, or small cans of juice, and it was pleasant because the old lady beamed even if we only spent twenty cents. In fact we didn't have to buy anything to earn her smiles. She could see me in the window from across the street and she would often wave and shout a greeting. She was always there and always alone. I never saw her go anywhere else.

Next door to the old woman's store there was a shabby house that had not been rebuilt since the big earthquake of 1976. An Indian family lived there. Their little girl was about four years old and was always dressed in the clothing traditional to her parents' village. The skirt had an elaborate design in an array of brilliant colors and was wrapped around her body and tied at the waist by a woven band. Her blouse had the traditional, identifying embroidery work. Sometimes she was barefoot, and sometimes she wore leather thongs. She was a miniature replica of her mother and looked as if she belonged in an exotic doll collection.

The mother had her own business—making tortillas. A big pile of firewood would show up on the sidewalk, and the family would haul it inside. Every day by mid-morning black smoke started rolling out the cracks, crevices, and doors of their house, and we could hear the slap, slap of her hands shaping the tortillas. Soon, people would begin drifting into the house with their baskets, bowls, and cloths to buy them for the noon meal.

Overall, the entire neighborhood was like a carnival all the time, a swirl of activity. Bus loads of children came to concerts at the conservatory. An Indian woman appeared daily with her assortment of vegetables, entered each house with her baskets, sat on the floor, and spread her goods out for inspection. Bells tinkled as the ice cream man pushed his cart down the street. Trash men came into the house with a drop cloth to bundle up the trash and haul it out to the cart. A flower lady came along with her huge basket each morning, and vendors sang songs praising and describing their wares. One man pedaled the street on his bicycle cart with huge containers of fresh milk and chunks of white cheese, which he sold to the women who hurried out to meet him with their jugs.

Because of this bustle and liveliness, I enjoyed stepping out the door each morning into the neighborhood. But most of all I enjoyed it because of the way people treated each other—smiling and extending courtesies that almost transformed our little community into a family.

Semana Santa—
Easter Week

*I*f I could name only one thing that Latin Americans have a special talent for, I think it would be their gift for celebration. There are countries in the world that have only a few national holidays each year and a few local ones, but you are not likely to find a Latin American nation among them. In Guatemala it seemed that holidays and celebrations were constant. Not only are there the expected array of worldwide religious holidays, Independence Day, and days to honor national heroes, but every village also has a saint, and each celebrates its saint's day with a week-long fair. At the very least, those of us in the project were expected to attend and participate in the fairs of Conacaste, Sanarate, and Monte Grande since they were in our municipality.

To select just one celebration as extra special out of the great numbers we had to choose from in Guatemala might seem presumptuous, but I would dare to name *Semana*

139

Santa, which literally translated means Holy Week. It is the week before and through Easter Sunday.

I think it is safe to say that nearly every living person in Guatemala goes on a trip or visits somewhere for at least part, if not all, of Semana Santa. Fighting our way onto buses during Easter week produced some hair-raising experiences. I especially remember the end of one Semana Santa when George and I were returning from Puerto Barrios by bus. Information regarding times and numbers of buses leaving had been sketchy. We had no choice but to wait and see. Next to one of the bus stations was a restaurant, where we had a cold drink while waiting. A woman who wanted to practice her English struck up a conversation with us. She had just put her son on a bus for Guatemala City, where he was enrolled in secondary school. While we chatted, the waiting crowd expanded at an alarming rate. Our new acquaintance noticed this and announced we would never make it onto the bus once it finally did arrive. But she had an idea. She invited us to come with her in her car out to a toll booth at the city limits. What that smart lady knew was that the buses coming into town to load up had to stop to pay the toll. That would give us a chance to talk our way onto it before it reached town and the big crowd waiting for it there. Twenty or thirty minutes later the bus rolled up. It was the kind used for cross-country travel, with reclining seats and wide windows that slide open sideways (great luck to have big windows as we would be crossing a desert area in midday heat, with no air conditioning). We talked the driver into letting us on, and after saying our goodbyes and thank-yous to the woman who had helped us, we sank into the exceptionally comfortable seats.

As we pulled into the bus station, we were astonished to see how much larger and more anxious the crowd had become. The second the bus stopped it was completely enveloped by the crowd. The driver seemed nervous and did not immediately open the door. Not to be deterred, people started climbing in the windows. Families and groups had apparently elected their most athletic member to climb aboard to save them seats. With a hand up and a shove from behind, people were wriggling in our window headfirst, tumbling into our laps. Not that they lingered there; they went scrambling immediately to claim the seats across the aisle that people coming in that window were about to grab. It was a free-for-all. We hung on to our seats and each other as we watched wide-eyed. When the driver finally opened the door, the competition for seats escalated. As people jockeyed for space, there were arguments over territorial stakeouts, of course, but fewer than I would have expected. The riders squeezed three or four to a seat, and if they couldn't do that, they grabbed one of the small wooden stools from the overhead rack and stationed themselves in the aisle. Within ten minutes the bus was solidly packed; not another person could be squeezed in, and we were ready to go. For me, the most surprising thing was how the people, with a few exceptions, remained pleasant and decent to each other in the midst of that chaos.

While Semana Santa is a vacation time for everyone in the country, Christians consider it their major religious celebration, a time for pilgrimages. In Guatemala a great percentage of the pilgrims go to the ancient city of Antigua, where one of the world's most famous reenactments of the Crucifixion takes place each year. Because it is so famous and in such a beautiful place, not only large numbers of Guatemalans come but hordes of foreign tourists as well. Knowing it was terribly crowded, most of us working in the project spent our Semana Santas elsewhere for the first two years. But by the time the third year rolled around, most of the tourists had been frightened away from Guatemala, so we decided it would be a good time for us to go to Antigua.

Antigua is a beautiful town of elegant Spanish architecture and cobblestoned streets, ringed by spectacular volcanoes. Whether arriving by bus, car, or motorcycle, you careen down a long, steep mountain road, with signs warning you to brake with your gears (and anything else you can think of). Upon reaching the valley, you enter the city and are greeted by a scene that has a Disneyesque quality to it.

Antigua was the first capital of Guatemala, but one day it was almost totally destroyed by an earthquake. Guatemalans are not people who give up easily, so they rebuilt Antigua, only to see it destroyed by mud slides when one of the volcano cones, filled with water from torrential rainstorms, gave way and spilled tons of mud down the mountainside. Residents dug out of the mud slide and restored the town, but this time the capital was moved to its present location in Guatemala City. The terrible earthquake of 1976 did great damage to Antigua as well as to many other parts of the country. Restoration of the city seems to be a continual task.

There are beautiful hotels in Antigua, some of them large and modern, others small and built around grass-and flower-filled patios, often with fountains in the center in the Old World, Spanish style. But for those of us on severely limited budgets there is the *pension*, a type of boarding house or inn. We had discovered a delightful pension during our visits to Antigua for Spanish-language tutoring. The landlady was a lovely person, and at $5 per day per person plus $1.50 for a big breakfast, the price was right.

Most reenactments of the Crucifixion around the world, except for those in Spain and Latin America, are done on a stage or in a church or perhaps in a great outdoor amphitheater. In Antigua the city becomes the stage, and the show is spread over days. In the appropriate sequence Jesus washes the feet of the disciples on the steps in front of the great cathedral in the plaza. A Roman soldier dressed in toga and breast armor rides on horseback through the streets and stops to read the proclamation of

142

the Crucifixion. The procession on Thursday evening carries the figure of Jesus kneeling in prayer in the Garden of Gethsemane. On Friday the processions depict Jesus' long march to Calvary, the thieves who were to die with him, and the Romans. On Saturday the processions of penitents continue, and at night a glass coffin, rimmed in gold and tiny white lights, with the figure of Christ laid out, is carried through the streets. On Sunday morning two separate processions move to meet each other in the plaza. One procession is composed entirely of men and carries the Christ. The other is all women, who bring the Virgin Mary.

The drama of the Crucifixion is the same wherever it is performed, although it may be presented in more elaborate and beautiful style in some places than in others. Guatemala does add one unique ingredient, a special kind of art form called "carpets." The carpets are not woven of threads; they are elaborate designs made of colored sawdust, flower petals, grains, seeds, chopped greens, and pine needles laid out in the streets.

In our pension the landlady's family occupied most of the rooms. They had come for both a family reunion and to make carpets in front of the house for the processions. In the front patio, stacked around the tile walks that bordered the flower garden, were washtubs, plastic bags, and boxes with the ingredients for making the carpets. Along with these were some planks, a number of two-by-fours, and wood stencils—necessary tools for the job.

After blocking off the street with sawhorses, some of the family swept the cobblestones. Next, they laid an outer frame of two-by-fours on the street, about twenty-one feet long and eleven feet wide. Then it was necessary to create a smooth surface over the cobblestones on which to make the design. A bed of natural color sawdust about three inches thick was spread and smoothed inside the framework of wood. Then the surface was covered with a layer of dark green sawdust. None of that was done quickly;

they took great care to make sure the surface was level and smooth enough. When they finally agreed that all was ready, they started to work on the border. The border design was elaborate, repetitious, and multicolored, containing a variety of ingredients. Four people with duplicate stencils started at the corners and worked to the right, filling in part of the design with colored sawdust. Another followed behind, adding a background of flower petals. The next person added seeds to form another part of the intricate design, and so on. Hours later they would remove the stencils and put on the outer edge trim of whole blossoms. Meanwhile, work had begun on the huge floral design in the center and the large designs toward each end. Planks were laid across the carpet, resting on the outer two-by-fours so people could crawl on them without disturbing the surface. It was a backbreaking labor of love that continued through the night and would have been sufficiently impressive by itself. But we discovered that they would create several more carpets on the same spot as each was in turn destroyed.

Around five on Friday morning, we strolled through the streets of Antigua to see the carpets ready and waiting for the processions. I don't have any way to do justice to the crisp beauty of an early morning in Antigua with the sun moving up from behind the volcanoes, but the beauty of the designs laid out that morning in the streets of Antigua made me feel that here was a moment in which people had created a beauty that outstripped nature.

Each carpet we came to seemed more beautiful than the last. Generally, those with the most delicate, intricate designs, similar to the designs used in oriental rugs, were made entirely in colored sawdust. Larger designs frequently made use of flower blossoms and other ingredients. One remarkable carpet extended thirty feet along the street and around the corner for another twenty and included a large variety of colors, styles, designs, and themes. Some of the artists were still putting finishing touches on their carpets as the first procession of the day was forming.

Thoroughly entranced by the carpets, we hurried on to see the procession start out. First came the Roman soldiers, dressed in either royal blue or crimson, velvet togas with matching plumes forming crests on the tops of their helmets. A few rode on beautiful horses, but most (a hundred or so) marched in a long line on each side of the street. After the soldiers came the penitents, devout men and boys dressed in purple robes. Any male who wished to pay the small fee, supply his own costume, and march for hours could participate as a penitent. Each penitent carried a tall wooden staff topped with a metal cross. In the middle of the street the drama was played out—the soldiers with whips, the thieves clad only in rags with the bars of their crosses roped to their shoulders as they staggered on their way to Calvary. Then, spaced at fairly wide intervals, came the larger-than-life plaster figures of the characters in the story of the Crucifixion. The figures and scenes were arranged on large platforms of polished mahogany, which were carried on the shoulders of more purple-robed penitents.

Each platform had long, heavy poles fit into the sides under the edges. There were notched and padded places on the under edges also. The men carrying the platforms could shift the weight from shoulder to hand as needed. Little platforms with a single figure could be carried by three men on each side. The largest, with several figures or an entire scene with plants and rocks, required fifty men on each side. Even then some of the men tired; penitents would periodically slip from the sideline to relieve the exhausted carriers, doing so one at a time to avoid any drastic weight change. One man led the platform at the front while another brought up the rear. Going around corners with the long platform was not easy. The platforms swayed and rocked, and the men shuffled backward and forward and from side to side as if in a coordinated dance routine. The lead men were dressed in white except for a purple sash and a purple headband holding their headcloth in place. The other men wore purple robes with white sashes.

The platform holding the Virgin Mary was carried by women who wore black dresses and black lace mantillas. The women lining the streets had also covered their heads with black mantillas, though otherwise they wore whatever they wanted. The day before, the women had worn white, but now that they were heading for the Crucifixion, they had switched to black.

As the procession headed toward the first carpet, I held my breath. I hated to see that beautiful piece of art destroyed. Those along the sides of the procession on foot or on horses passed easily between the edge of the carpets and the curb lined with marching penitents. The small platforms also moved easily along the sides. But when the big platform with Jesus came, it was carried straight down the middle. Given its size, no other choice was possible, and, in any event, the carpets were designed specifically for Jesus and the Virgin Mary to "walk on." Thus, as we watched, all those hours of labor were wiped out. But then, once the entire procession had passed, the artists rushed out into the street with brooms to clean up the mess and start over again to create another carpet for the next procession. The people in our pension made five different carpets for Semana Santa. Of course, the first set of carpets were more elaborate because of the amount of time available to make them, but they were all beautiful.

When people wanted to make a "quickie" carpet, they laid a thick base of pine needles and then made very large designs using whole flower blossoms, large pods, and so on. Sometimes that type was made in a different shape also—perhaps round or oval.

Another facet of the processions was the band made up of beating drums and wailing brass. Though it wasn't a jazz band, I was reminded of New Orleans funerals as I listened to the music. In each procession, a band marched directly behind the platform carrying Jesus, and sometimes there was a smaller band behind the platform of the Virgin.

I was struck by how deeply involved the people were who participated in this Semana Santa celebration. I watched an old woman push through the line of penitents to wave burning incense in front of the Jesus figure as she wept and asked for mercy and help. I watched fathers and sons, mothers and daughters walking for miles and miles as a symbol of their faith. The processions wound through the city hour after hour. I was swept along by crowds passing into the plazas and entering churches to view the carpets in front of the altars, to light candles, and to buy tortillas, sweets, and balloons.

On Saturday afternoon after wriggling through masses of people to follow a procession, I finally sat down, exhausted, on a shady curb at the edge of the main plaza. The procession had moved on, as had most of the crowd, though many people were still wandering at random, eating ice cream cones and cotton candy. As I sat there, an Indian family decided they liked my spot in the shade too and sat down beside me. In fact, they surrounded me and seemed ready to absorb me into their lives, at least temporarily. They were making balloon birds to sell. The whole family worked at it. Only the nursing baby and a toddler were exempt. They blew up balloons, twisted and tied them, glued on wings, and painted on eyes. They were speaking Spanish and sitting practically on top of me. A meandering tourist caught my eye. She was a young Oriental woman and her attire was unusual. She was wearing an odd-looking man's felt hat and a shirt tied around her middle. But what was really eye-catching was the item that was more or less covering her bottom. Even rather conservatively styled shorts are somewhat startling to Guatemalans outside Guatemala City and certain resort areas. What this young woman was wearing were white, short, draped shorts open up the side to the waist. She was clearly a tourist, easily identified by the camera around her neck, the sun lotion visible through the sides of her net bag, and the sunglasses and map, to say nothing of the brochures in her hand telling her about Guatemala. I was just wondering to myself what Guatemalans would think of her outfit when the father of the balloon-selling family answered my unasked question. I heard him snicker, poke his wife in the ribs and say, "Look! Look at that crazy lady wearing a diaper!" I laughed out loud before I could catch myself. I hadn't meant to let them know that I understood what they were saying, but they didn't mind at all. The wife giggled. Their eyes twinkled, and they seemed amused to share their observation. I spent the next half-hour in pleasant conversation with them before I wandered on.

The procession on Saturday night was perhaps the most beautiful of all. The long lines of penitents carried candles, the platforms were lighted, and the glass coffin outlined in tiny white lights was dramatic. The streets and plaza were tightly jammed with people.

We were in for a surprise the next morning, however. We went back to the plaza expecting the same huge crowds. After all, it was Easter morning and in the States that had always been the most important time in the celebration. In our Congregational church in Evanston, we had special services for Maundy Thursday and Good Friday, but the high point was the glorious celebration of the Resurrection on Easter morning; and my Roman Catholic friends and neighbors engaged in equal, if not bigger, celebrations. Therefore, we were startled to find only a little gathering of people in the plaza. A small procession of men garbed in purple and white and carrying Jesus moved to meet an even smaller procession of women (now dressed in white), carrying the Virgin Mary. Priests and acolytes were swinging the censers. A bishop gave blessings and went through some kind of ritual that we were unable to hear or understand. As the processions joined and headed for the cathedral, we departed with a friend for Guatemala City to attend services at a Guatemalan Protestant church. As we left, we had cause to wonder if the ceremony of Semana Santa, with its Crucifixion, didn't represent the ultimate affirmation of the importance in this society of dying a noble death. The celebration of the Resurrection appeared almost to be an afterthought.

The Pope's Visit

I would like to recommend to mayors and city planners everywhere that if they have a dream of cleaning up and rejuvenating their cities, they start by issuing an invitation to the pope to visit. The coming of Pope John Paul II to Guatemala City caused a transformation: buildings were repainted and refurbished; construction projects were speeded up; street and sidewalk repairs took half the usual time. The giant cathedral on the main plaza was repainted, including its exquisite trim work, rimmed with lights, and dramatically spotlighted. Private homes as well as public buildings were beautifully refurbished. And it didn't make any difference whether the pope was likely to see it or not. The fixing, cleaning, and refurbishing went on throughout the entire city.

As the arrival date drew nearer, the frenzy increased. Suddenly, all the curbs in the city were turning white. Groups of students, neighborhood residents, and others simply appeared with brushes and buckets to paint them.

Next came the trees and light posts, which were painted either white or gold from the ground up to a height of four or five feet. Where there were long lines of trees or posts, the colors were alternated. It was not uncommon in Guatemala to see trees in some of the parks with their trunks painted white partway up, but the addition of gold was something new, and so was the experience of seeing painted trees and posts everywhere.

Then huge banners and bunting and signs of welcome began to appear on buildings all over town. Last, came the construction of huge arches of palms and flowers stretching across the streets and boulevards at intervals along the route the pope would pass in the official procession. Intricately designed carpets of flowers, petals, seeds, grains, and colored sawdust, like those we saw in Antigua during Semana Santa, were laid along the way.

Even if a person were not interested in seeing John Paul, it would have been worth a trip to Guatemala City to watch the people who had come to see him. Obviously, it was not only Catholics who turned out for the occasion. The police had to warn people to be wary of the thieves that worked the crowd. Security in general was tight. It would have been a special horror if any harm had come to the pope in Guatemala (at least it was a time of relative peacefulness with Rios Montt in the palace). The visit was an historic occasion because no pope had ever visited Central America before.

I was surprised to learn that the pope, when he travels, must stay either in a bishop's residence or in the residence of the apostolic delegate to the nation he is visiting. (When formal relations exist between the Vatican and a nation, the apostolic delegate is not only a papal representative but has diplomatic status as well.)

The problem of arranging for John Paul's sleeping accommodations made for a rather curious and rigorous schedule. He would stop first in Lisbon and then go on to Costa Rica, then to Nicaragua on March 4, though he would go back to Costa Rica for the night. On March 5, he was scheduled to go to Panama, then back to Costa Rica to sleep. On March 6 he would go to El Salvador for the day and arrive that night in Guatemala. He was to spend the next day and night in Guatemala and go to Honduras on March 8, returning to Guatemala to sleep. Departure ceremonies from Guatemala were to be held at the airport on the morning of March 9. He would stop at the airport in Belize only to say mass, before leaving for Haiti.

On the morning John Paul was to make his procession through the city, we were out early. Masses of people had gathered in the streets and in the Central Plaza in front of the palace and cathedral. The scene reminded me of a cross between Mardi Gras and the Rose Bowl parade. It was a sunny day and the city was sparkling. The arbors of flowers in the park were showing off with an extra burst of color. Pope John Paul was to enter his "Pope-mobile" in front of the cathedral, circle the plaza (two blocks in size) and turn down Sixth Avenue. We had decided it would be impossible to get near enough to see him in the plaza, so we waited on Sixth Avenue nearby. The street was very narrow there, so everyone who gathered along the sidewalk was guaranteed a close look.

We knew when the pope had entered the plaza by the cheers, which rose and moved in a wave around the plaza, coming closer and closer to us. Then suddenly there he was, right in front of us, not fifteen feet away, standing in his "Pope-mobile." I had a glimpse of dazzling white robes, a smile, a raised hand as he whizzed by, tearing through the carpet of flowers. The vehicles must have been going almost thirty miles an hour, which is surprisingly fast for a procession. Although the fast pace was probably an important part of the security plan, it was disappointing to have him fly by so quickly. Still, we were lucky to have been close enough for a fairly good look at him. He was scheduled to say mass at the huge military parade ground an hour later, so we hurried off to join the crowds waiting for him there. Traffic was closed off in the major streets where the pope had passed, and we walked down the middle of boulevards under beautiful arches of palms and flowers. Thousands of people were flowing toward the parade ground and wading through the remains of the flower carpets. Vendors were everywhere, selling food and souvenirs.

Nothing could have prepared me for the sight of the parade ground. The grassy earth was covered with a carpet of human beings. Off in the distance a wooden platform and altar had been constructed. People had spread out blankets in some sections and were sitting on the ground. Other areas were solid with people standing. Many had radios, which was the only way to hear what Pope John Paul was saying because there was no sound system available that could reach over the distance.

An old tank, put to rest on the parade ground, was covered with people. I was told later that a newspaper somewhere in the world had printed a picture of it with a caption that indicated tanks were necessary to "keep the peace," as if that old rusty tank would have been of use for anything other than a decoration. It reminded me of the old cannons often seen on courthouse lawns in small towns in the U.S.

We wriggled our way through the crowd but never got close enough to see the pope very well again. It was fascinating, though, to study the faces of the people. Many wore expressions of rapture, and almost everyone seemed to have entered into the festive spirit of the day.

The by-product of the visit of Pope John Paul II was the sparkling city, complete with parks that looked like fairylands. It took quite a while for the paint—and the spirit of that day—to fade.

Of Elections, Bombs, and Coups d'Etat

Coups d' état are a fact of political life in Latin America— though they are not, of course, the whole of politics in Guatemala. Historically, Guatemala has had a pattern of fairly regular elections, most often involving more than two political parties in competition.

During the time of the Conacaste Project Consult in June 1978, Guatemala was preparing for the inauguration on July 1, 1978, of the newly elected president, General Lucas. As usual, the losing parties claimed the election had been dishonest, and tensions were running high. As a consequence, we foreigners endured our first body frisk. Our team from the consult, which was studying the business and economic aspects of the situation in the village, set forth by bus one day to visit some factories and businesses in the area. The team was a mix of villagers and foreign consultants, and I must admit we were a somewhat strange-looking conglomeration of people. As we entered Guatemala City to tour a fabric factory, the police flagged us down and ordered us to get out. The women had their passports or other identification checked and were lightly and quickly frisked by policewomen. The men were given a more thorough check by the male officers. They were lined up with feet spread, arms out, and palms against the side of the bus. We were permitted to return to the bus a few at a time, after it had been inspected. Some of us pulled a young Peruvian colleague away from the window as he leaned out to photograph the frisking procedure. We didn't want to embarrass the police or increase their nervousness.

The government managed to contain the preinauguration tension. General Lucas took charge and kept control until March 1982, almost his full term of office.

During the last eight months of the Lucas regime, conditions in Guatemala became more and more violent. The kidnapping, torturing, and killing by the "White Hand Death Squad" was on the increase, and if not supported by the Lucas government, it clearly was not being stopped by them. During the same period of time, the guerrilla (leftist) activities had expanded. It was hard for ordinary people to decide if they had more to fear from the left or the right. Indeed, it was difficult to know for sure which atrocity was being committed by which side. Sometimes government soldiers would enter a village disguised as guerrillas. The guerrillas, in turn, often disguised themselves as soldiers when they attacked. Meanwhile, those of us on the scene were horrified by the picture of the Guatemalan situation that was being painted for the rest of the world through the news media. Whatever the reality was in Guatemala, the reporting of it was extremely inaccurate, even twisted, yet stated with absolute authority, as if the people in the U.S. and Europe knew more about what was going on in Guatemala than the people who lived there.

For those of us working in the project, the last few months under the Lucas regime were the most frightening times we lived through. The poor Indians in the outlying villages were caught in the middle. The guerrillas would knock on their doors and tell them they must provide food and support or be killed. Then the army would come along and tell the same people that if they gave support to the guerrillas they would be shot.

The guerrillas didn't need to fight an all-out war. They bragged instead about having plenty of patience and time and did not hide who they were or what they were about. Their strategy was simple and very smart: to create fear and damage or destroy the economy. In a country where a great portion of the economy is dependent on tourist trade, that is a relatively easy job. Plant a few bombs around the city, tell horror stories around the world, and the tourists flee. (It is probably counted a special victory if you can maneuver the U.S. into putting out a travel advisory.) When the tourists stop coming, the first people hurt are the ones who are waiting tables and changing beds in the posh hotels and the ones who earn their livelihood by the skill of their hands: weaving, carving, or making silver jewelry and elegant leather goods. These people make up an important part of the economy because they earn the foreign currency needed by developing countries. Big business (including the hotels) and governments can hold out for quite a while, but the ordinary people go under fast. Therefore, when the tourists stay away, they are doing exactly what the guerrillas want them to do. (Fortunately, on a return visit in January 1987, I discovered the tourists had returned to Guatemala in large numbers.)

When the bombs first started going off in the city, it was clear they were not intended to kill people but to destroy property, create fear, and demonstrate the ability of the guerrillas to get away with it. They were not trying to alienate the masses of Guatemalans; they blew out the windows of shopping centers and skyscrapers and knocked out power stations. They also broke into prisons and released hardened criminals, hoping to create more problems for the government by increasing the crime rate. Shoot-outs, attacks on the power stations, and car chases went on at night. Consequently, during those last months of General Lucas's term of office, the streets that had buzzed with activity in the evenings were deserted by eight o'clock. Movie houses and restaurants were empty, and sidewalk vendors who had done a booming business now faced financial disaster. The spirit of the city seemed to change. We hurried inside too, whenever we were there.

We did, however, experience some close calls, along with the rest of the people. I remember walking on a city street with George one day when I noticed a beautiful house. I tugged at George's sleeve and pointed it out to him. A plaque on the gatepost identified the building as the Spanish Embassy. We stood for a moment and admired its architecture before we went on. A little later that day it was the scene of a shoot-out and fire in which several people died. Diplomatic relations between Spain and Guatemala also died as a result of the incident.

Early one morning, George and I set out to meet John Turton, the general manager of Xerox. The Xerox offices were located on two floors of the twenty-story Chamber of Commerce Building. It was one of the new, modern examples of architecture in Guatemala City, located on its own triangular plot of land, with streets close beside it on three sides. In front was a busy boulevard; the streets at the sides of the building were more quiet and were used for local traffic and parking.

We had agreed to meet Mr. Turton at 6:45 because we were to begin a seminar with the sales force at 7:30. The main entrance would not be open that early, so we had agreed to meet at the underground garage entrance in the back of the building and go up together in the elevator from the garage. We knew there would be no problem parking beside the building at that hour.

We arrived early and were about to pull in and park

when we decided instead to drive down the boulevard to the Pancake House for a cup of coffee rather than sit in the car and wait for ten or fifteen minutes. When we returned to the building, what a shock! Only a few minutes earlier a carload of explosives parked beside the building had blown up. It was one of the guerrillas' favorite tricks— parking an old car (usually stolen) filled with explosives beside what they wanted to destroy or damage and setting it off with a timing device. The damage that can be done by a carload of explosives has to be seen to be believed. There was a huge crater in the street where the car had been. If we had been parked where we had started to pull in, there is very little chance we would have lived through it.

The glass in the building had been blown out. The steel window frames had buckled, and windows and roofs were destroyed in nearby smaller buildings also. The area was crawling with army and police personnel. We parked and walked to the building, terrified that John Turton might have been caught in the blast. But as we approached, John came running to us. He had arrived just after the blast. He asked us to go up to the offices with him to assess the damage. Not trusting the elevator—even if it had been operating—we started climbing up the eleven flights of stairs to the Xerox offices. We were ankle-deep in shards of glass all the way up. Unfortunately, it was a windy day, and with all the windows gone, it was a battle to hang on to briefcase and banister while shuffling through the glass without being blown over. Office walls bulged out into the hall, water was running down them from burst pipes, and giant plants that had been ripped from their pots added dirt, leaves, branches, and pot fragments to the crushed glass. Paper was scattered everywhere. If anyone had left important papers on a desk the night before, they were gone now. Some of the inside doors had been blown out of the building.

Walking into the Xerox offices was a special shock because we were so familiar with them. Within the past two weeks we'd had several meetings in the conference room with its floor-to-ceiling windows overlooking the city, the mountains rising beyond. Now it was totally destroyed, with wind howling through the blown-out walls.

The three of us wandered around, picking things up off the floor and surveying the damage. George told John we would be happy to help in any way possible, but he assumed Xerox would want to reschedule the seminar. To our surprise John said, "Oh, I think we might as well go ahead and begin; there must be some place around here where we can meet."

Maybe we shouldn't have been surprised that John was eager to move ahead. We had facilitated a successful seminar a few months earlier for the company, and they were eager for in-depth training in participatory planning. Xerox in Guatemala was experiencing a problem which they shared with many of the multinational corporations there. The American and other foreign general managers and upper-level executives had been pulled out, as their various home offices began to get nervous about their safety (especially after the American general manager at Goodyear, who had been kind enough to donate tires for our old VW pickup, was kidnapped and murdered). The companies suddenly found themselves with staffs that were almost entirely Guatemalan. In many respects this was great for the companies and good for Guatemala, except that the top executives at home often felt uneasy at the speed with which the Guatemalans had been catapulted into higher positions with less than the usual preparation. The need for more skills in participatory management and planning emerged almost overnight. ICA, with years of experience in applying the participatory planning methodology, was seen as a valuable resource for these businesses. We selected a small, windowless inside room and started shoving chairs into it. The salespeople were arriving, so we all pitched in to set up the room and bring some order out of the chaos. The room was long and narrow and, with everyone there, much too crowded, but we still had a good first session.

What we were doing was consulting with the Xerox sales staff to help them figure out how to meet the stiff competition they were getting from Canon, which had somewhat demoralized them. With our guidance they developed a creative plan and time line, along with a new sense of being a team, which drove up both morale and soon thereafter, sales (sales doubled over the next two months).

I was amazed during this initial meeting at the attentiveness of the Xerox staff and their ability to participate in the midst of the banging and scraping of the cleanup and repair. It struck me that each time people don't fall into hysterics, each time they pick up and go on in the midst of frightening and threatening situations, each time they take control of a situation, they win a battle against the terrorists.

Considering the violence that was going on in various places around the country, it was strange that out in Conacaste (fifty-four kilometers from Guatemala City), you would not have known there was anything happening. In El Progreso, the state in which Conacaste is located, life was normal and peaceful. I remember hearing only one story of guerrilla action in a village in El Progreso. Because the land was more desertlike and had few trees and virtually no forests, it was not easy to find hiding places, which perhaps made it less attractive to the guerrillas.

The danger in which those of us who worked in organized development projects lived was made very clear to us by the experience of our friend, Padre Burke, who had worked in an Indian community for many years. The focus of his project was on creating the least expensive and most attractive houses possible. The project had developed some fine models. Padre Burke had also become interested in applying some of the ICA methodology in comprehensive community planning. As a result of our interest in

161

each other's work, we had spent time together exchanging ideas and information. It was obvious that the people in his community had great respect and affection for him, though others clearly did not. One night the mutilated body of one of the project participants was dumped on Padre Burke's doorstep, with a note attached saying the priest would be next unless he left the country immediately. Padre Burke left Guatemala, and it must have broken his heart because he loved the country and the people and considered Guatemala his home. We only learned what had happened after he had gone.

Even though we did not feel we were in direct danger, we remained very much on the alert and did everything possible to protect ourselves. In addition to keeping a low profile, I checked in regularly at the American Embassy for a briefing on the situation as the embassy staff perceived it. We were also in constant touch with our Guatemalan contacts, especially in the business world.

During the almost six years we were in Guatemala, this was the one period of time (September 1981 to the coup in March 1982) when we felt a full-scale revolution might actually occur. Consequently, we tried to keep the gas tank in our old VW pickup topped off, and I went to the Mexican Consulate as frequently as necessary to keep the visas of everyone on the staff up-to-date. Mexico was the closest safe border if we ever felt the need to jump in the car and get out fast. Also based in Mexico were other ICA staff with whom we had been working, so it was a natural place for us to go. At that time our Conacaste staff consisted of people from Venezuela, the Philippines, Guatemala, the U.S., and India. This degree of national diversity meant we would not be allowed to leave on an American evacuation ship in the event things got that bad, so the Mexican border would have to suffice.

During that period of time, with the possibility of revolution hanging over us, there were admittedly some frightening moments. A number of projects were threatened, and most of them pulled out. Many individuals working in development assistance were recalled. The number of nongovernmental organizations similar to ours remaining in Guatemala dwindled drastically. The Peace Corps pulled people out of areas they judged to be unsafe, an action that proved to be to our benefit, as we inherited a fine young man who was a great help on our demonstration farm.

National elections were held on March 23, and the new president-elect was General Angel Anibel Guervara Rodriguez, of the same political party as President Lucas. There were strong grumblings regarding the honesty of the election, but we were not prepared for our first experience of a coup d'état (*golpe de estado*).

George and I didn't experience the coup firsthand because we were working in Mexico City at the time. The moment we heard the news, I phoned the U.S. Embassy in Mexico to inform them about our international staff working in Guatemala and to ask for an evaluation. They explained that our embassies don't talk directly to each other but through the State Department in Washington. They promised to contact Washington and call me right back with an appraisal of the situation. They did so within a half-hour. The information was incomplete but basically reassuring. The airport was closed but was expected to open the next day, and there appeared to be no violence and no reason why we could not return by bus as planned. They recommended that we keep trying to call friends for firsthand information, but they didn't believe we would have to evacuate our staff. After a couple of hours we were finally able to talk with friends in Guatemala City. They laughed at our anxiety and said everything was fine. It seems people had gathered on the streets and rooftops near the palace to watch the changing of governments, as if they were observing the changing of the guard at Buckingham Palace. So on March 23, 1982, a triumvirate of young military officers took charge of the government. On

May 28, one of the three, General Rios Montt, became chief of state. On June 12, 1982, the general was declared president. What was most striking was the fact that an established government had been smoothly replaced in a few hours, and within a few months a man had been declared president—without benefit of either violence or elections.

From our perspective, President Rios Montt was a considerable improvement over President Lucas. Obviously, the coup that eventually put Rios Montt in power was of great interest to us. We watched hopefully and, for the most part, were not disappointed. If his religious fervor seemed excessive to many people, it was balanced by his campaign for honesty in government, which he promoted through posters, TV, and newspapers. It was a refreshing change. When the president created the Council of State in early 1983 to advise the government, we were amazed at some of the foreign criticism leveled at him because the members of the council were appointed rather than elected. President Montt had made an honest effort to see that the council was representative of the people. Indians appeared in the government for the first time, though they were required to speak fluent Spanish (the vast majority of Indians speak only their own languages). Selecting the Indian council members through an election would have taken months, if not years. There were some outstanding, nationally respected people on the council, and we thought it was an excellent first step. Two of the appointees were long-time friends and supporters of our project. Both had impeccable credentials: one was an attorney, Lic. Ricardo Umaña, who had given many hours of free legal service to the project; the other was the nationally renowned director of Children's Hospital, Dr. Asturias Valenzuela, who also served many years with CARE.

One day a front-page newspaper story reported that the government was handing out thousands of guns to villagers and giving them training so that they could form

home guards to protect their communities from harass-
ment by guerrillas and radical right groups. I was excited
by the thought that the government had decided to trust
the people to that extent since the guns could have been
turned against the government. I figured Montt was fairly
shrewd, handing both beans and bullets to the hungry
people. It seemed he must have calculated his risks carefully. Imagine my shock when I returned to the United
States and saw a film which depicted this man as some
kind of monster, forcing villagers to form home guards.

We found many constructive and significant activities
received practically no recognition in the international
press. During this same period, for example, we collabo-
rated with two friends of President Montt. They worked
without pay in tandem with the Comité de Reconstruccion
Nacional (National Committee of Reconstruction or CRN)
and nongovernmental agencies such as ours. They were
involved in the resettlement of Indian villages and the supply of food and medical services to outlying areas. We
knew of their work, not only by what they told us, but by
what was reported to us by the American Embassy and
CRN. Their work was never reported outside Guatemala,
nor was that of CRN.

The CRN was established after the terrible earthquake
of 1976, when the world rushed to the aid of this small
country. That was wonderful, but no nation can simply
open its doors and allow people and materiel to pour in
totally without control. CRN took responsibility for the
distribution of the donated goods and held the nongovernmental groups accountable for what they said they would
do. It has continued over the years to play an effective,
nonpolitical, regulatory role in Guatemalan economic development, but it is seldom mentioned in the news outside
the country. In my opinion, it has been an important ele-
ment in helping stave off violent revolution.

CRN has managed to maintain a surprising degree of
political neutrality in the midst of the turmoil. It is in a

unique position; groups like ours had the option of signing a contract of agreement with CRN or of working independently. That is, it was possible to remain in the country doing some kind of development work without an official relationship with CRN, but it might attract curiosity and suspicion from various quarters. Our Guatemalan advisors, especially our lawyer, Mr. Umaña, recommended drawing up the agreement and signing it, which we did. Basically, the agreement described our plan for the coming year, stating exactly what we expected to accomplish and when. In return, CRN provided assistance and advice. When we needed special kinds of expertise, CRN helped find it. That was an achievement when you consider that a major part of the ICA development philosophy was to connect local people with local resources. If CRN knew of special services or materials available from government sources or from elsewhere, we were informed. When we had people, like the Iowa group, from other countries bringing loads of donated materials and tools with them, we notified CRN and they arranged for everything to be whisked through customs rapidly and duty free. When our visas were due for renewal, our request to CRN brought forth a letter to the authorities so that we had only to drop off the visas for the officials early in the morning and pick them up in the afternoon—no waiting in lines, no hassles. (You have to have worked in a foreign country to appreciate the value of that service.) If the police stopped us in one of their spot checks for weapons or explosives, the CRN card presented with the driver's license almost always saved us time. We were given some preferential treatment because of our CRN identification, but not because we had pull. It was more an expression of respect and gratitude to people who were directly helping the poor.

CRN had no funds to distribute, and its own agency budget was quite moderate. This no doubt helped to keep it honest. Its employees were dedicated and caring people who wanted to serve their country. They worked not only with foreigners and Guatemalan government agencies but also were in constant contact with committees from villages, advising them on locally developed projects such as setting up a health clinic. CRN was in continual contact with the Guatemalan people. Anyone—peasant or gentry—could walk in off the street and expect a courteous response to a request for information or advice. Thus, CRN had the respect and affection of great numbers of people, including Indians and Ladinos. Obviously, it behooved both politicians and guerrillas to think carefully about their public relationship to CRN. An open attack on the organization could touch off an angry reaction from the large number of people who depended on CRN for practical help.

With President Rios Montt in the palace, the spirit of the city revived, and life returned to the streets and parks. Nights were gay again. It seemed as if the nation exhaled a great sigh of relief and returned to its normal routines. "Honesty in government" became the slogan of the day. CRN staff worked hard to restore the stability of village life. Refugees returned in large numbers, and in the spring of 1983, amnesty was offered by the government to any guerrillas who wished to lay down their guns and go home. Many took the government offer and returned to farms and families. We occasionally heard stories of guerrilla action in distant villages, but violence was drastically reduced, and there were no more bombs in the city. One obvious sign of the time was the massive replacement of glass in Guatemala City, which once again sparkled in the sunshine. The ending of the attacks on the power stations allowed the city to regain its old nighttime sparkle too.

One of the more unusual aspects of this period was the instigation of two-hour Sunday afternoon sermons, delivered by the president on TV to the entire nation. President Rios Montt was a born-again Christian, dedicated to evangelism. The *evangelico* movement in Guatemala had been gaining in strength and numbers long before the coup d'état, but with an evangelico in the palace, the momentum picked up. Large groups of North American evangelists began arriving in Guatemala. Great numbers of them were based at the Pan American Hotel in the city, moving out from there to the countryside, where they preached, baptized converts, and helped build new churches in the villages. They brought money into the country and were no doubt sincere and dedicated to their mission. Unfortunately, their presence brought criticism down upon the president. Many people were displeased with his support of the evangelists and with some of his public statements that Roman Catholics found insulting. One involved a reference to a large gathering of evangelicals in the city's stadium. The Catholics, Montt said in effect, couldn't pull together that big a crowd. It was a bit of braggadocio that did not sit well in this predominantly Catholic country. Maybe the pope didn't like it either; when he came to Guatemala some months later, he won the "numbers game" hands down.

We heard stories through the grapevine that some of the generals went to the president to demand that he muffle his support of the evangelical proselytizing that was going on if he wished to remain in the palace. It was said that he agreed to their demands, but in fact nothing changed; and a few weeks later in August 1983, George and I missed a second coup.

We had attended an ICA international meeting in Chicago and had stopped to visit my parents in Florida for a few days while waiting to catch a ship out of Tampa, a cost-cutting device we used when we dared take a little extra time. So once again, we were outside of Guatemala, getting the news reports over the phone. Only this time our staff had its own little side drama going on, which in the telling sounds more like the plot of a Mack Sennett film than real life.

To start, it's necessary to back up a little. Over many months consensus had been building in our staff that we needed a computer. For one thing, we were close to being buried under paper as we tried to keep up with the reports required by IADB for the loan. A word processor and printer would help us produce copies in English and Spanish. The bookkeeping aspects of managing the loan, plus our own accounting, curriculum development, and training programs also made the idea of a computer attractive. In addition, we felt it might be possible to help support ourselves by selling our word-processing skills. After many months of effort on the part of one of our staff members, the joyous news was announced that we were to be the proud owners of an Apple computer, a letter-quality printer, and several packages of donated software to be sent in from the U.S. A hitch in communications with customs caused a delay, but at last one Friday morning in August it arrived at our office. Our office in the city, just two blocks from the palace, was supplied free by José Luis Betencourt, S.A., a company that sold and serviced Apple computers. The owners (father and sons) had been good enough to give us the use of their old office space when they moved into new quarters around the corner, though they retained use of the first floor. The offices consisted of four nice-sized rooms and a bath on the second floor and were quite adequate to our needs. In order to enable ICA and Betencourt to operate wholly separately, we decided to construct a new door opening directly to the outside. The Betencourts hired a carpenter to do the work. When the computer arrived, the numerous boxes were carried in through the Betencourts' office and up to ours. The Apple was partially unpacked so that everyone could "ooh" and "aah" over it, and then left there. What no one knew was that the carpenter had decided to work on Saturday, and, unfortunately, he did not complete his work. He did carve the hole in the wall for the new door, but then he nailed a few old boards across it and went home.

On Monday morning when the first staff members arrived at the office, they found it totally stripped. Not only was the Apple and all its components gone, but so were the electric typewriter, the new manual typewriter, the paper supplies, and the clothes people kept in the office to change into when they came to the city. Even our battered coffee pot and hot plate were taken. The thieves had also found a set of car keys someone had left in the office. We immediately called the police and a locksmith, who would come out and change the locks on the car.

So it was that on August 8, 1983, detectives were standing in our office taking notes for a report on the robbery while a locksmith worked on the car. Suddenly everyone became aware that something was going on outside. People were running up the street, away from the plaza. One man had a bloody head. A helicopter flew down the street at roof level with soldiers hanging out, automatic weapons at the ready, looking in the windows at my colleagues. Another coup was under way.

The detectives turned pale, gasped, and said, "Something is happening. We must go," which is exactly what they did. The locksmith had apparently removed the locks without a problem until he got to the ignition. That proved difficult, so he decided to remove the steering column and carry it with him back to his shop. Unfortunately, when he entered the plaza with this odd-looking cargo, he encountered a group of soldiers who thought he was carrying a machine gun. It is probably just luck that instead of opening fire, they ordered him to halt and throw down his "weapon"—which he was happy to do.

Within a few hours a new government was settled into the palace. Once again power had changed hands by way of a coup d' état, and once again, no one was killed. (Both Lucas and Montt still live peaceful lives in Guatemala, coming and going as other citizens, sometimes visiting the United States.)

Nothing seemed to change appreciably with the new government. The new chief of state (not president) was General Oscar Humberto Mejia Victores. He immediately disbanded the Council of State. However, over the months, preparations were made for elections, and in September 1984, a new Council of State convened with newly elected representatives for every department (into which Guatemala is divided for electoral purposes).

The most important issue with regard to elections, as I see it, is that in a sense Guatemala is not one, cohesive nation. The Indians, living in their villages, speaking their own languages, wearing their own special clothing, following their particular ancient customs (including their own version of Catholicism), and maintaining their own tight-knit community, perceive themselves more as members of their people than they do as Guatemalans. So in a sense, there are more than twenty nations in Guatemala. The government (including the regimes that came to power while I was there) has been working to forge a unified country from these diverse groups. The task is not an easy one.

The result of the continual political brouhaha is that most poor Guatemalans don't care who is in the palace. They will shrug and tell you it doesn't make the slightest difference who is in charge. What they really want to do is live in peace, farm their land or do their job, and give their children a better chance in life than they had.

If the Guatemalans do have an image of the right kind of leadership, it appears to me to be mixed up with the old *patrón* image. The patrón is the boss. His is the final word. And of course, if the people turn themselves over to the patrón, they are in a sense his slave. At the same time, they can avoid the burden of making decisions and taking responsibility for what happens in their lives—and blame

171

the patrón for everything that goes wrong. This image of the patrón carries over into the business world. I have had more than one general manager in a multinational corporation tell me he has a terrible time getting his Guatemalan executives to make the decisions they should be making at their level. Many seem to do almost anything they can to defer decisions to the top person.

Those of us working in the project could identify readily enough with the general managers, as we too were constantly struggling against the patrón image. The villagers kept trying to force us into the role of patrón—to make the decisions—and the mistakes. In particular, they wanted George West (as project director) to be the patrón. It appears that deep down, the average Guatemalan, if given a choice of government, would prefer a benevolent dictator—a phrase used consistently by people ranging from village council members to national government officials to describe their favorite president in history, Jorge Ubico.

Most of the people held the cynical opinion that anyone in top government was, as a matter of course, going to rake off as much money for himself as possible. The Ladino population of our village considered President Jorge Ubico an exception to this rule. Ubico, who had been president during the 1930s and 1940s, had confiscated land from the previous president, who had, in turn, confiscated it from the owner. The land had been a large *finca* (plantation), and the peasants who had worked for the landowner lived in one area of the finca, forming the village that became known as Conacaste. When President Ubico took over the land, he did something revolutionary with it—he gave it to the peasants. In 1933 an announcement was posted, explaining that the peasants could file a claim for a piece of the land.

Don Juan Campos, one of the few Conacastans who could read at that time, saw the notice and made haste to notify the other men of the village so they could register a claim. Consequently, the majority of the families in Conacaste today own small parcels of land. Ownership means the land can be passed from father to son, and land can be sold to someone else in the village if he will live there and use it. Owners are permitted to sell to someone outside the community only after the land has been offered for sale to every landholder in Conacaste. Title is held through a special government agency which checks the papers and procedures every step of the way. The regulations serve as a protection for the people who lack the education and sophistication needed to protect themselves from the unscrupulous. It is also a system that guards against return to the giant fincas controlled by a few very rich people. There are still some large fincas, but these days they are more benevolent, usually providing jobs, homes, schools, and health clinics for the resident workers. I personally know of one finca where the peasants threw out the guerrillas when they came around causing trouble. They were satisfied with their situation and had a strong sense of loyalty to their employers.

While President Ubico was popular with the peasants of Guatemala and even with its middle class, he was not popular with right-wing political groups; and he was certainly not popular with the United States, where, I gather, he was labeled a communist. President Ubico remained in office from 1930 to 1944. He had been elected to office but was overthrown in a coup that installed a more conservative government. Most Guatemalans firmly believe that the U.S. government supported that action.

Memorial to Esteban

*E*steban showed up in Conacaste on loan from another non-ICA project to help us with the construction of a large bakery oven since he had had previous experience in the construction of ovens. We were impressed by his capacity for hard work and his tenacity. He was not a loquacious young man, but when he spoke, he appeared to be intelligent with a serious turn of mind. Esteban had a lean, sinewy build and the muscles of a farmer. He was relatively tall for a Guatemalan, with medium-dark skin and thick black hair framing a somewhat long face with high cheekbones and an aquiline nose. He sported a mustache, which I suspect he may have grown to partially hide a scar on his upper lip. He was clearly of the Mayan Indian heritage, something of a novelty in Conacaste, a community of Ladinos.

Esteban had been with us about three weeks when he finished the oven and was ready to leave. We had been sufficiently impressed with his work to invite him to remain on a more permanent basis. After several conversations and some careful thought, he accepted.

Esteban stayed and worked for us and ultimately fell in love with another staff member. She was a young woman of Conacaste who had worked with us from the time of the consult and who was raising her little boy alone. Their romance had its ups and downs. One of the more dramatic downs occurred after a quarrel. The woman had said she would not marry him and had walked out. From a neighboring room, I suddenly heard someone shouting that Esteban was in the bathroom with a carving knife, threatening to kill himself. I rushed to him. He must have wanted to be stopped, for otherwise I would not have been able to outwrestle him for the knife. This kind of drama was not unusual in Latin America. Great emotions in the arena of romance are common. I was told that sometimes there were almost epidemics of young men throwing themselves off the high bridge that we crossed to leave the city, killing themselves because of unrequited love.

Anyway, the lovers talked things out and finally made the decision to marry. From the viewpoint of their families and the village, it was a mixed marriage. Historically, the Guatemalan Indians were proud of their Mayan heritage, continuing to embrace the old customs. Marriages tended to stay within the village or tribal area. The Ladinos, on the other hand, were prejudiced against the Indians, though the degree of prejudice varied according to area and situation, being worse in the city than the country. I never witnessed any hostility or unfriendliness in Conacaste toward the couple, but that doesn't mean it didn't exist. There were no problems we were aware of, and certainly nothing that affected their work in the project. Esteban seemed to be well liked. At any rate, it did take a certain degree of courage for the couple to go against cultural traditions.

To my sorrow, I missed participating in the wedding

as I was in the States at the time, but the event was described to me when I returned. The wedding was held at Esteban's home near Chimaltenango, and everybody seemed to have been very impressed by its loveliness. I'm sure it was different from a Conacaste wedding as the Indian personality and style are not the same as the Ladino. Several months later, I had the opportunity to meet Esteban's parents and talk with them when they visited Conacaste. They were small in stature but were people of great dignity.

The day came when Esteban and his wife had a baby girl. Esteban was the epitome of the proud father. He glowed at everyone.

In time the responsibility and cost of raising their two children, plus the desire of Esteban's family that he join them in farming, brought them to the decision to return to Chimaltenango. Though we understood their decision, we were sorry for it, and we were concerned about the area of the country to which they were returning. Violence had been on the increase around Chimaltenango, both by guerrilla and government forces. But most of us, to maintain our sanity, put such fears in the backs of our minds and assumed that terrible things would only happen to people we didn't know.

I had tucked away my anxieties and had vague plans to go up to Chimaltenango for a visit someday. It was upon our return from a meeting in Venezuela several months later that I was given the shocking news of what had happened to Esteban and his family while we were gone. George received the news ahead of me and was kind enough to withhold it until we were alone at home. When he told me what had happened, I burst into tears from the shock and horror of it.

It seems that Esteban was with his parents and one sister in their house when a group of armed men showed up. His wife and the two children were in the other house a little distance away. No one will ever know who the men were, why they were there, or why they did it, but they simply opened fire on the family. They slaughtered Esteban, his mother, and his father and left his sister for dead, though she was only wounded and played dead to survive. When Esteban's wife heard the shooting, she stayed hidden with the children. The killers, who could have been guerrillas, radical right fanatics, or common criminals, stole the family's vechicle and fled. The family had not been involved in any kind of political activities insofar as we knew. The reason for the murders will probably remain a mystery forever. Unfortunately, Guatemala is full of such mysteries.

What kind of person was Esteban? He was serious much of the time, but when he laughed, he sparkled. Underneath a quiet and dignified exterior lay deep emotions. The day I wrenched the knife out of his hands, he fell into my arms and sobbed. He had a wondrous way with children and had accepted his wife's first child as his own, clearly without reservation.

I liked Esteban. I especially remember the fun we had trying to find our way around Mexico City on the subways during a two-week assignment there in the early months of the project. Our relationship reminded me of an elderly couple I had known during my childhood in Evanston. The woman was nearly blind, and her husband could barely walk. She used to tell me what a fine pair they were because "she was their legs and he was their eyes." Esteban and I operated somewhat that way. My Spanish was weak, and Esteban was not sophisticated in the ways of a big city. We developed a kind of symbiotic relationship.

Esteban's death was a tragedy and a waste. He had no special political beliefs; he wasn't a revolutionary. Esteban is a symbol of all the ordinary people trying to live decent lives in peace while contending political factions use them like pawns on a chessboard. This kind of tragedy has happened a thousand times over everywhere in the world. This time it was in our own backyard.

And how did we honor our friend who had been killed? We went on with the work of the project—our memorial to all the Estebans of the world.

Dust unto Dust

*I*n the very early days of the project a number of us non-Guatemalans got into a discussion about how to "get inside" the people of a nation and culture other than one's own. George West was part of that discussion and expressed his theory that one of the best ways to understand how a particular group of people think about life is to study how they think about death. He pointed out that the attitudes people have regarding death directly and strongly affect how they live their lives. He also suggested we find out whom the nation regards as heroes and martyrs (which also relates to how they died).

I am grateful for having participated in that discussion because it caused me to be sensitive to and aware of things going on around me in Guatemala that I might otherwise have failed to understand. It caused me to ask questions that I might not otherwise have thought to ask—questions that produced some revealing answers.

One of our early observations was that many Latin

American heroes (not just Guatemalan) were people who might be labeled losers by North Americans. They were the valiant leaders who had struggled mightily to save their nation from invaders but had lost. Nevertheless, they had invariably been beloved leaders, great warriors, and most important, they had died nobly in an effort to serve their nation. Dying nobly was ultimately the most important. We began to see that in Latin American literature, music, and films, the embracing of death with dignity was a recurrent theme. Whether one died on a battlefield or in a city hospital or a mud hut in a village, it was clearly important to die with dignity.

I learned a great deal about death in Guatemala from a friend, Rolando, who came from a poor family but had managed to attain a good education and had worked his way up into the middle class. I asked him about the *Día de los Santos* (All Saints' Day) that is celebrated on November 1 each year. A group of us foreigners had gone to a cemetery in Sanarate on Día de los Santos to learn more about it.

Every year, during the week before the celebration, our Guatemalan staff members would request time off to go to the cemetery to paint the tombs of deceased family members. The cemeteries all over Guatemala were centers of activity as people poured in with brushes and buckets of paint. Most of the tombs were above ground, cement vaults in the style of those in New Orleans in the States. I've never been sure why they were above ground because none are built on marshland as are the cemeteries in New Orleans. Quite the contrary, it may have to do with rocky, hard soil. At any rate, the vaults are the prevailing custom. The bodies are slipped in the end of the tomb and the opening is sealed with cement, where names, dates, and other information are inscribed. Some of the tombs are single while some may be very large and have space for several family members. Almost every cemetery I saw in this country (except for the first one in Guatemala City) was colorful. The cemetery in Sanarate had tombs of hot pink, bright aqua, lemon yellow, mint green, and every other color you can think of. A few tombs were painted white but not many. Frequently, they had niches where flowers could be placed—most often plastic bouquets. Some of the graves were in the ground, but most of those were completely covered by a cement slab which could be painted.

On Día de los Santos itself it seemed as if everyone in the country visited the cemeteries. At the Sanarate cemetery vendors collected at the entrance, selling food, flowers, and mementos. People gathered at the tombs, where they took turns talking to the deceased. For the most part, the visitors appeared to be cheerful and relaxed. In addition to talking with each other and to the deceased, they decorated the tombs with flowers and wreaths and in some cases with paper streamers as well. Only one person seemed sad, a woman who stood sobbing in front of one of the tombs. When I approached close enough to read the inscription, I understood why. It had been only a few days since the death of her loved one.

One sight that gave me a strange feeling (because it was so contrary to what I had learned was appropriate behavior in a cemetery) was seeing visitors spread picnic lunches out on the ground beside the graves or, when the tombstone was flat, on the grave itself, using the tombstone as a table.

My Guatemalan friend, Rolando, explained that this visit to the cemetery is an important ritual for Catholics. Its purpose is to feed the dead and tell them what has happened in the lives of the family during the time since their last visit. The food they bring is called *fiambre,* which consists of a platter of cold meats, cheeses, and vegetables. I had noticed many signs in city restaurants advertising fiambre for the Día de los Santos. Special sweets of Indian origin are also customary.

Rolando told me that if someone died in an automobile

accident, a cross would be placed by the side of the road at the death site, and the family would also visit there and decorate the cross just in case the soul of the deceased had not come to the grave with the body. (On bad curves or where a bus had gone off the road, there were sometimes twenty or thirty crosses, a vivid reminder of the virtue of safe driving.) I had the impression from our conversation that in addition to honoring the soul, the more superstitious might believe that the soul would cause them trouble if they didn't honor it properly.

Probably the most important point Rolando made was his explanation of the Guatemalan attitude toward death. One accepts one's fate, composing mind and body and preparing loved ones for the inevitable. Rolando insisted that because of the importance they place on dying with dignity, most Guatemalans have no fear of natural death. When I think of what I witnessed of death and the reaction to it in our village of Conacaste, I have to accept his statement as true.

My first experience in Guatemala with severe illness— which came early in my stay in Conacaste—was repeated many times. When urged to go to the hospital for help, the sick villager would almost invariably respond, "Well, but it is quite possibly my time to die, and I wish to die in my home with my family around me." I never sensed fear in that statement. We foreigners seemed to be the ones who were fearful.

Whenever a villager died, there was an all-night vigil during which the village laymen, who looked after church affairs, said the rosary. The deceased was placed in a plastic body bag in a pine-box coffin (which was then closed out of sensitivity to those present, because of the warm climate and because there was no embalming). Chairs and benches were set up facing a photograph of the deceased, with a great display of fresh flowers, greens, and palm leaves surrounding it and lighted candles in front. This altar might be in the home, though it was often outside, in which case the men usually built up an area roofed with palms around it. Whether inside or out, a thick carpet of pine needles was spread on the floor or ground. Sometimes plaster figures of the saints were borrowed from the church to enhance the altar arrangement.

Once the rosary was completed (it could take an hour or more), the women of the household, assisted by friends from the community, served coffee and tamales to everyone present, which normally took a long time because of the limited supply of plates and silver, which had to be washed for successive servings. When the meal was finished, people played card games or visited quietly. There was rarely much crying, even by the immediate family. The exception was in the case of the death of a child or a young person—and then most likely only by the closest of relations. People expressed their sadness at having lost someone they liked and worried out loud how they would manage without the loved one or friend—a practical question when it came from a widow with small children and no income.

The next morning the coffin was carried to the church for a special service. Again the villagers would say the rosary, pray, and sing songs. The service was led by a layman since almost no family in our village could afford to pay the priest to come over from Sanarate to say a mass. Then some of the village men would pick up the coffin and lead the procession to the cemetery. Villagers would join in the procession as it passed. The family and a good many villagers would walk the seven kilometers to the cemetery, up and down the winding mountain road, frequently in ninety to one-hundred degree heat. Later, as the economy of Conacaste improved and more vehicles were available, families sometimes hired a pickup truck to carry the coffin. Anyone not joining in the procession was expected to come out in front of the house and stand respectfully by the side of the road as the coffin and procession passed. When the church bell tolled, our staff would leave our work and stand respectfully by the road, and one of us would join the procession as a matter of courtesy. We could not have expected the villagers to respect the work of the project if we had not been ready to respect their customs.

On the anniversary of each death, the family of the deceased conducted a ceremony similar to that of the death vigil but somewhat more celebratory since this event ended the year of official mourning.

When I tried to sort out what I had heard and seen regarding the cultural attitudes toward death in Guatemala, my mind went spinning off in different directions. On the positive side, the Guatemalans' fatalism, combined with their religious faith and the customs and celebrations which surrounded death, clearly helped them face death without fear and be at peace with themselves. It also enabled them to accept and survive the harsh conditions of poverty in which they lived.

On the negative side, the fatalistic acceptance of the condition of their lives made it harder for them to believe themselves capable of making changes. The implications of that attitude were clearly a constant challenge for the work of the project. We were nurturing them and nudging them toward making decisions and taking responsibility for making plans and shaping their own future, but their deeply imbedded attitudes toward life and death made some aspects of our work more difficult.

I found that understanding this attitude toward death was very helpful; it enabled me to communicate and work with my neighbors more effectively and to understand the meaning of some of the things that were said to me. I never stopped urging people to try to save lives whenever it was possible, but knowing how they felt and having respect for their position (and a certain degree of admiration) gave me clues as to how to approach each situation more effectively and with less danger of giving offense.

What More
Could We Ask For?

*D*uring the consult the people of Conacaste had created their own four-year comprehensive plan. By the third year of the project, when many of their goals had been achieved, the staff decided to do a survey of future priorities among the villagers, which meant meeting the villagers individually in their homes to discuss the matter with them. Approximately fifteen hundred people call Conacaste home. That comes to a few more than two hundred households. But since the village is divided into five sectors, it was easy for each of us to take part of a sector and sally forth in pursuit of the community will.

I was glad to be back with the villagers again, having spent most of my time before then on fund-raising assignments in the city. I was delighted to see the new babies and old grandparents, to talk about the crops, the children, newly acquired TVs, new construction, new romances, new jobs.

So into the houses I went—houses of cement block,

adobe, sticks and mud, or just sticks and a little cardboard; houses with aluminum roofs, palm roofs, tile roofs; walls decorated with calendars (with scenes of Colorado, Mexican bullrings, gringo babies, dogs and cats, blonde movie stars, bare-breasted ladies, and saints with halos), along with family pictures, crucifixes, bunches of garlic, printed prayers, messages from the evangelicos, and ads for batteries.

At each house I was invited in and given a seat on whatever they had. If there were no chairs, it might be a wooden packing box, a bed, or a hammock. I was always offered some refreshment, most often coffee, loaded with sugar that I didn't want and that people could not really afford. I drank the coffee anyway because it was a gift, generously given. I admired the children and expressed gratitude for the fine refreshment on such a hot day. Then we would try to talk about the future. Once again, I would discover how difficult it is for people out of a long history of poverty to dare to dream, especially to dream out loud.

That lesson was driven home to me most emphatically in one of the poorest houses in the community, built entirely of sticks. My hostess greeted me with a warm, toothless smile as she dumped a child and cat off a wooden box and seated me. As we visited, she made her tortillas and kicked the chickens and pigs out from under her feet. We talked about the change in the village, and she expressed her pleasure in having a light in her house and clean water nearby. Then I asked her what she thought we should work on next. She looked completely baffled, so I tried asking the question another way. On the third try, she finally understood. She grinned, waved her arm to indicate her surroundings and said, "But we have electricity and water, what more could we ask for?"

Epilogue

*A*fter leaving Conacaste, George and I lived in the U.S. for several years and then joined a new ICA project in Peru.

When I first went to Guatemala I think I expected to serve as a volunteer for a year or two and then return to the U.S. and work in real estate. If, on the other hand, I decided to continue in service work, I thought I might want to go back to school for more specialized academic training. I had no expectation of a long-term relationship with ICA, nor had I ever considered living and working in community. Also, I had begun the relationship to ICA by paying them for the privilege of being a volunteer, and that obviously could not continue indefinitely. But as time went on, I became so deeply involved in the work I did that I simply could not see myself working at anything else. And it was not simply a feeling of doing good.

My greatest culture shock has always come when I return to the U.S. I do not particularly wish for the rich to have less—only for the poor to have more. Neither am I arguing that everyone needs to be equally well-off. Whenever I return to be with the "haves," I am wined and dined and royally treated—and I love it. My husband made an enlightening remark to me once when I had crept away from the project one weekend for a bit of luxurious living in the city. Knowing I was feeling guilty about it, he said, "Why should you feel guilty? Of course you enjoy a hot bath, good food, a glass of wine, and no fleas in your bed. Everyone enjoys a little comfort. Anyone who tells me otherwise is either an idiot or a liar. Enjoying the luxuries of life is only a problem when it becomes the meaning of your life." My experience in Guatemala led me to the discovery I could move back and forth between these two worlds, making a clear distinction between them and knowing with certainty that physical comfort and pleasure were not the meaning of my life.

As I mentioned earlier, I used to get very uncomfortable when people called me a saint just because of my decision to work in a service vocation. But the idea of being a saint took on a different meaning when I learned what the word meant originally. It simply meant a single-mindedness of purpose or the focusing of one's whole life on a particular vision. With that definition I can say, yeah, well, maybe. But it is clear in my mind that there is nothing especially noble about working in a project or living with the poor. I live with the poor out of free choice. At any moment it would have been possible for me to make a new decision to walk away from the poverty. I was not trapped in it as they usually were. My experience in Conacaste has taught me to be very conscious and intentional about making decisions. I made the conscious decision to live the rest of my life doing work that will help bring about a better world.

But the form of my compassion and the way I conceive of a better world have changed. I have had, for instance, to harden my heart to the beggars on the street. I have come to grips with the fact that even if I had enough money to give every poverty-stricken person in the world a dollar that would not touch the underlying issues which permit poverty to exist. At best I could only postpone their deaths by a day or so. This has been a hard fact for me to internalize. I have generally leaned in the direction of being a bleeding heart, so it isn't easy for me to brush aside the beggar who sticks the stump of his arm in my face or to ignore the starving baby who is shoved at me by a pleading mother. It is painful, but I have conditioned myself to walk away and to give all that I have to working on long-term solutions. (There are those who achieve a great deal by working on short-term solutions, and that's good, but it's not my way.)

The value I have found in ICA and what initially drew me to it and to the kind of work I was doing was that it was long-term. It rejected the idea of giving people something for nothing or offering "band aid" development. That, we at ICA believe, is the surest way to destroy a group of people because it deprives them of initiative, responsibility, and sense of self. Seeing those qualities grow is one of the principal joys of the work, more so than receiving gratitude for helping. If you enter development service looking for expressions of gratitude, you'll almost certainly be disappointed.

But I cannot deny that what was happening inside me was as important as what was happening in Conacaste. I think what I learned most about was pain. As I grew close to these people, I appreciated more and more the strength and courage they displayed in dealing with pain while at the same time living rich, full lives. I am better able to accept that pain is as important a part of life as pleasure—and that's a new idea for me.

So you see, in the end, I can't say I have sacrificed myself on the altar of doing good for humankind. Yes, I feel that what I am doing will help large numbers of people create a better world for themselves and make the world

191

a better place. But what I did and am still doing is what I feel at home with. Certainly I will return from time to time and savor the pleasures of affluence, but then I'll go back to work with people who are striving to pull themselves out of their poverty and reap some of the benefits of the modern world. I can hardly think of living any other way.